Henri Stierlin

Photos: Anne and Henri Stierlin

HINDU INDIA

From Khajuraho to
the temple city of Madurai

TASCHEN

KÖLN LISBOA LONDON NEW YORK PARIS TOKYO

Page 3

A magic diagram

This *yantra* comes from an un-published Rajasthani manuscript dating from the eighteenth century. The product of a system of thought deriving from tantrism, it is a cosmological diagram symbolising creation in magical form, and is intended as an aid to meditation. (Musée d'Ethnographie, Geneva)

Page 5

A Chola bronze

The praying figure here is Rama; when thus portrayed with an axe, he is known as Parashurama. The work was cast using the lost-wax process and is typical of the bronze sculptures made under the Chola dynasty of southern India. Production continued after the heyday of the dynasty (A.D. 836–1267), lasting into the seventeenth century. (Musée d'Ethnographie, Geneva)

© 1998 Benedikt Taschen Verlag GmbH
Hohenzollernring 53, D-50672 Köln

Editor-in-chief: Angelika Taschen, Cologne
Edited by Caroline Keller, Cologne
Co-edited by Carola Nerbel, Heidelberg
Design and Layout: Marion Hauff, Milan
English translation: Chris Miller, Oxford

Printed in Italy
ISBN 3-8228-7649-6

Contents

INTRODUCTION

A Religious Architecture

A triad: Vishnu, Lakshmi and Devi
Set between Fortune and Prosperity, the four-armed god Vishnu displays his attributes: conch shell, solar disk, lotus flower and mace. The three bronze figurines are set within an arch symbolising the temple. Southern Indian in style, they date from the seventeenth–eighteenth centuries. (Musée d'Ethnographie, Geneva)

Hindu architecture is one manifestation of the intense spirituality of the vast country that is India; it is an expression of a religious faith whose rites are a daily presence in the lives of millions. Temples are found everywhere in India, in town and country alike, and bear vivid witness to the devotion of the many religious communities to their protean divinities. These wonderful monuments form a rich and varied contribution to the Indian cultural heritage.

Many of the buildings erected in medieval times to meet the needs of Jain and Hindu rituals still survive. Between the fifth and eighteenth centuries innumerable temples were constructed, some hundreds of them on a very large scale. On all sides we find places of worship and sacrifice, some carved into the rock, some excavated, some built in conventional fashion, and all dedicated to the disconcerting Hindu pantheon. These monuments, intended to attract vast crowds of worshippers, are a universal phenomenon in India.

Unlike the churches and cathedrals of the Christian West, which were designed to accommodate crowds of believers in a collective ceremony, Hindu sanctuaries are primarily designed to accommodate the statue or sacred emblem of the divinity. Indian religious monuments do not, for the most part, contain large internal spaces. They are 'tabernacles', preceded by halls used for ritual, music and dance. The temples are often decorated with ornaments and sculptures illustrating the great myths of the Hindu pantheon.

It is the development and function of these architectural forms and their abundant decoration that constitute the subject of this study. We do not propose to set out either a repertory of the 'styles' of India or a description of the infinite variations in plan and elevation of the temples. Rather, our aim is to define the meaning of these ornate structures. It is to decipher the message expressed in Hindu temples and interpret the meaning of the effigies, sculptures and ornaments that animate their sacred architecture.

We hope in this way to cast light on the sources of Hindu architecture, which remain obscure. Hindu art is one whose origins are, all too often, beyond the reach of scientific investigation. We shall analyse the forms of extraordinary masterpieces, the organisation of a rich iconography and the programme behind a form of sacred town planning. Under this scrutiny, Hindu art is revealed as less exotic than at first sight it appears.

Our research has taken us on an extensive tour of the peninsula, and to twenty of the most sacred places of Hindu worship. Our analysis covers some fifty monuments built over the course of more than a thousand years, starting with cave sites that date from the first centuries A.D. and ending with the sacred cities of southern India that were built as late as the seventeenth and eighteenth centuries.

Geographic Conditions

India is often referred to as 'the subcontinent'. There are two reasons for this: first, its immense size; and second, its almost total isolation from its neighbours.

In the historical sense of the word, 'India' referred to the territory bounded by the Hindu Kush and the Himalayas, and extended from modern Afghanistan and Pakistan in the west to Bangladesh in the east. South of the basins of the Indus and Ganges, rivers whose sources lie in the mountain barrier to the north, India includes the entire peninsula: the Deccan. This lies between the Gulf of Oman and the Bay of Bengal, projecting like a triangle into the Indian Ocean. Its surface area is five million km² (about sixteen times the size of Great Britain). But the India covered in this book is the peninsula itself, that is, some two million km². This is the area bordered by Rajasthan and Gujarat to the west and by Bengal to the east and comprises the whole of the Deccan. It is situated almost entirely between the twenty-fifth and tenth parallels and traverses the Tropic of Cancer.

The monsoon climate affects the entire country, bringing torrential rain every year. This is important to agriculture; with the exception of the Indus and Ganges in the north, there are few rivers, and year-round irrigation is rarely possible.

The isolation of the subcontinent derives from its physical geography. India is almost cut off from the world around it. In the north, the mountains form an all but impenetrable barrier to approach from China, while the Indian coastline was out of reach of its neighbours until the advent of long-distance navigation. The Deccan is, moreover, flanked by mountain ranges, the Western and Eastern Ghats, which constitute a natural barrier.

The temples of Khajuraho
A hymn to the gods, the medieval masterpieces of Khajuraho, raised on a huge podium, lift their towers into the radiant blue sky. Dating from the eleventh century, the Kandariya Mahadeva Temple, left, and Devi Jagadambi Temple, right, are separated by the little Mahadeva sanctuary.

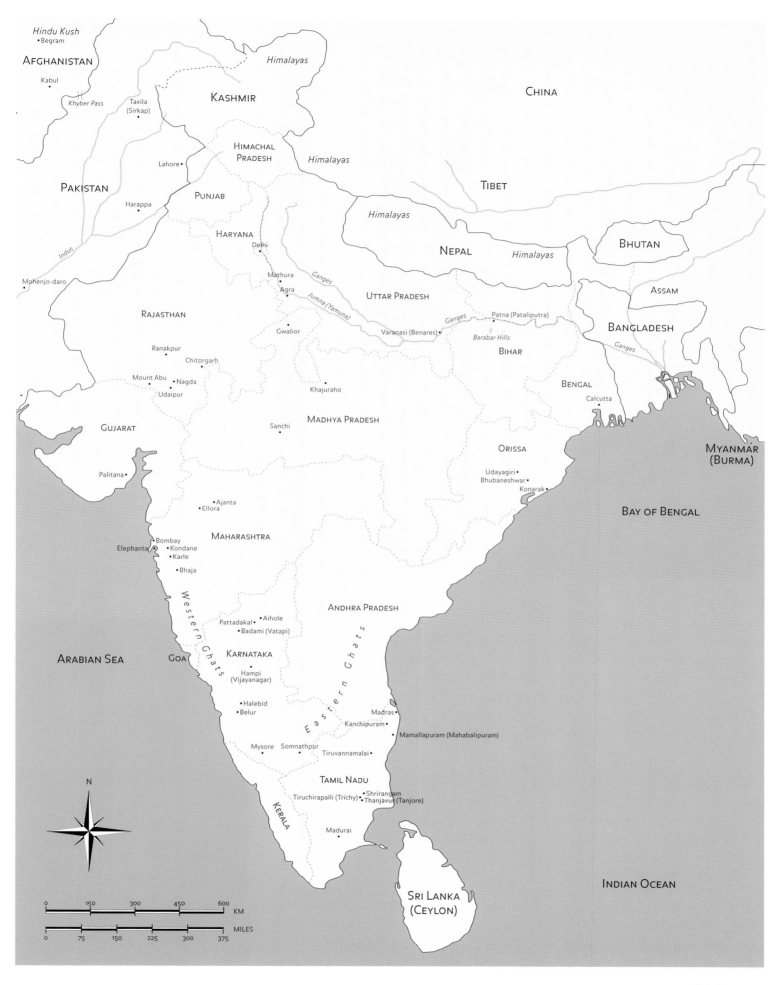

The only land route into India has always been a difficult and perilous one, that of the Khyber Pass, which leads over the Hindu Kush, reaching an altitude of 7 600 m. Through this north-west passage have come several waves of immigrant peoples and invaders. And the major influences on the art and culture of India have followed the path of the merchant caravans and conquering hordes, trailing over the mountain passes before descending into the fertile plains of the Indus and the Ganges.

Among the movements of peoples and civilisations by which the Indian world has been enriched, we should first mention the successive waves of Aryas. The Aryas were Indo-Europeans who settled in India in the second and first millennia B.C. Then, in the sixth century B.C., came the Achaemenid/Persian conquest of the north-west of India. That was followed by the campaign of Alexander the Great, thanks to which the Hellenistic Bactrian kingdoms bequeathed certain elements of Greek culture to the empire of Ashoka (third century B.C.). This Greek influence was particularly noticeable, for example, in the treatment of the human figure by the Buddhist sculptors of Gandhara.

Though the Arab invaders of the eighth century entered India as far as the Indus through the deserts of Baluchistan and Sind, the Khyber Pass was the channel through which the Islamisation of India took place. The Turko-Afghan invaders of the end of the twelfth century were followed by the hordes of Genghis Khan in the thirteenth century and by Tamerlane's Mongol cavalry in 1398. In the sixteenth

The exaltation of beauty
Following a tradition that dates back to the *toranas* of Sanchi, nymphs (*surasundaris*) disport themselves beneath sculpted branches or palm-leaves. This figure comes from the exterior of the Rajarani temple in Bhubaneshwar and dates from the twelfth century.

century, one of his descendants, Babur, who came from Fergana, established the Mughal Empire. This eventually covered almost all of India, and ensured its unity prior to the British conquest.

The World of the Aryas

The Aryas (or Aryans – the name is unfortunately associated with the racist myth of the Nazi Third Reich) were a white people of Indo-European origin. In the second millennium B.C., they made their way down in successive waves to the remotest plains of the Indus and the Ganges. The peoples who retreated before the Aryan advance were Dravidians, people of dark skin and straight hair who had at some time in the very distant past left behind their Ural–Altaic origins to settle in India. It is thought that they had themselves displaced Australoid aborigines, who occupied most of prehistoric India.

The Aryas came from the plateaux of Iran; they were a pastoral and semi-nomadic people, whose tribes began their migrations between 1300 and 1100 B.C. At this time the cities of the Indus civilisation, Mohenjo-daro and Harappa, were already destroyed, probably around 1600 B.C. These cities had been founded in the third millennium B.C. by a remarkably well-organised society, which was in many respects comparable to that of the Sumerians of Mesopotamia. The Indus script has defied all attempts at decipherment, and we consequently know little about the civilisation.

By 1100 B.C., the Aryas were using iron tools. They had domesticated the horse and could use the swing-plough. They were therefore in a position to increase their pressure on the native peoples of India. The Aryan settlement of India took place over a very long period, between, say, 1300 and 800 B.C. With the Aryas came Vedic, an archaic form of Sanskrit, a language related to Iranian and connected with Greek, Latin, and the Germanic, Scandinavian and Celtic languages – in short, with the vast Indo-European family.

The beliefs of the Aryas are essentially based on the four *Vedas* (meaning 'knowledge'), which set out the Vedic religion practised by the *brahmins*. From this ancient religion Hinduism emerged early in the first millennium, after suffering an eclipse during the rise of Buddhism. These Vedic texts are among the most important literary monuments of the second millennium B.C. They include the *Rig-Veda*, the *Yajur-Veda*, the *Sama-Veda* and the *Atharva-Veda*. Brahminical literature would add to each of them the *Brahmanas*, the *Aranyakas* and the *Upanishads*.

The four *Vedas* seem to date back to the period during which the Aryas were settling in the plains of the Indus and the Ganges. The *Rig-Veda* is a book of hymns to the various gods. The *Yajur-Veda* consists for the most part of sacrificial formulas, while the *Sama-Veda* sets to music sections of the *Rig-Veda*. The *Atharva-Veda* brings together a large number of magical and divinatory texts.

The *Upanishads* are a later addition to this basic corpus. Most sections of the *Upanishads* are datable to between 500 and 400 B.C. This mass of writings, piously preserved by a tradition dating back over a thousand years, comprises thousands of verses constituting the foundations of the Vedic religion. The linguistic similarities within the Indo-European group are reflected in the clear analogies between the Vedic pantheon and the Greco-Latin and Germanic mythologies.

The divinities of Vedic India are innumerable, and their functions frequently overlap. Simplification is inevitable. The essential deities are Mitra and Varuna, who represent day and night; Dyaus Pitar (Zeus the Father) is a sky god; Indra, the king of the gods, wields the thunderbolt and puts demons to death; Vishnu, destined to become the supreme deity of Hinduism, reigns over space and traverses the universe in three strides; Agni, the god of fire, presides over sacrifice and over the liturgical flame and the domestic hearth alike; and finally, Soma, the force of life, personifies the sacrificial potion that bestows immortality, and is a major liturgical divinity.

Human sacrifice was phased out early in the Vedic religion, but animal sacrifice was required and followed a meticulously prescribed procedure. This was particularly true of the most important ritual, the royal sacrifice of the horse, which the sovereign was required to perform under certain circumstances; it affirmed the magical power invested in the king.

Already in Vedic time, Aryan society divided into four classes forming a strict hierarchy. The *brahmins* were the priests, who alone were capable of performing the complex rituals of the Vedic religion. The *kshatriyas* were the warriors, who held power. The *vaishyas* were cattle farmers, peasants and merchants, on whose production Aryan society depended. Last came the class of the *shudras*, or manual labourers, the origin of the Untouchable caste. The hierarchy established by the Aryas gave rise to the Hindu caste system, which proliferated in endless subdivisions.

It seems that, in the ancient Vedic religion, a temple was not required for sacrifice; that could take place on an open-air altar built specifically for this ritual. Archaeology has little to tell us about the Vedic world, and there are no identifiable remains of temples or architecture in general from the high period of the Vedic civilisation.

Absence of History

The fact is that, between the destruction of Mohenjo-daro and Harappa (about 1600 B.C.) and the development of the first Indian cultures under Chandragupta Maurya (circa 320 B.C.), there is an archaeological black hole of 1000 years. We know nothing about this period. And the Vedic texts, which are of religious inspiration and present a cyclical time-structure, provide no historical evidence. A concern for chronology probably arrived in India with the Achaemenids and the Greeks, first seen particularly in inscriptions. Prior to that there are neither lists of sovereigns nor local or regional chronicles of a European kind. Hence the almost total absence of historical landmarks by which events may be dated or a notion acquired of the development of Aryan civilisation.

Historical consciousness might be said to arise in India during the reign of Ashoka (269–232 B.C.), the third king of the Mauryan dynasty. His capital was Pataliputra (present-day Patna) and from it he dominated almost all the peninsula with the exception of the southern Deccan. Profoundly influenced by the Hellenistic kingdom of Bactria, he had his edicts engraved in Greek, Aramaic and a variety of Indian languages. These engravings are found both on rock faces (in the Achaemenid manner) and on columns of a form and construction similar to those of Persepolis. The columns seem nevertheless to have been erected and engraved by native sculptors rather than by the Greco-Persians, to whom they were long attributed.

The symbol of Shiva
In the dark sanctum of the Shivaite temple, the *linga* symbolises the creative power of that protean deity. The faithful anoint the head of the linga with offerings of ghee and flowers. This little linga, sculpted in black schist, dates from the eighteenth century. (Musée d'Ethnographie, Geneva)

Shiva's cosmic dance
Encircled in flame, Shiva Nataraja, the lord of creation and destruction, enacts the dance of the endlessly changing universe. This superlative bronze was cast under the Chola dynasty of Thanjavur and dates from the twelfth century. (National Museum of India, New Delhi)

The Emergence of Hinduism

In a society devoid of historical narrative and events, it is difficult to specify the development by which the ancient Vedic religion eventually gave rise to a series of rejuvenated cults such as those that appeared at the dawn of the first millennium. At some time in the sixth century B.C., there would seem to have been a reaction against the excessively rigorous ritual requirements of the Vedic system. The founders of the reforms introduced by Buddhism and Jainism were individuals of the *kshatriya* families, in other words of the highest classes: Mahavira Jina (Mahavira the Victorious) and Siddhartha Gautama the Buddha (the Enlightened One). Together they put an end to blood sacrifice with their emphasis on an ethical view of religion. This reform was put into effect in Hindu religions too.

Hinduism took most of its deities from Vedism. And the Aryan contribution to this renewal was evident. The Hindu doctrine was called *arya dharma* (the Aryan or aristocratic order). Doctrine is perhaps not the correct term for the mass of sometimes mutually contradictory precepts produced by this rapidly evolving religion. The texts from which Hinduism drew its most important inspiration were the *Brahma-Sutra* and the *Bhagavad Gita*, the latter of which was included in the great epic poem, the *Mahabharata*.

The *Brahma-Sutra* is a summary of the Vedic teachings of the *Upanishads*, and came into being between 200 and 450 B.C. It mainly concerns knowledge of *brahman* and *atman*. In the *Rig-Veda*, *brahman* refers to prayer and hymnody, while in the *Upanishads* it means 'the first cause of all that exists', that is, the foundation of the universe. This is contrasted with the notion of *atman* or 'universal soul', which was soon transformed into the eternal principle of individuality, the 'self'. The debates in Hindu philosophy turn on the dialogue between *brahman* and *atman*, since it is the outcome of this dialogue that decides the future of the individual.

While it is true to say that the main gods of the Hindu pantheon derive from Vedic sources, it is important to take account of the profound transformation that each of them underwent in this process. Thus Vishnu became one of the major gods. The notion of *avatar* is important in Hinduism; the word *avatar* refers to a kind of 'incarnation', a life on earth. And one of Vishnu's *avatars* is the Lord Krishna, the hero of the *Bhagavad Gita*. Krishna is first and foremost a warrior; he is also a founder of cities and an exterminator of demons. Subsequently he becomes the divine shepherd and guardian of souls. In this amiable form, he courted his wife Radha, and the courtship imparts an element of erotic mysticism to his legend, which is endlessly recounted and embroidered.

Another *avatar* of Vishnu is the god Rama, who is inseparable from his wife Sita. He is the hero of the *Ramayana*, which tells the tale of his combat with the demon. It is startling to find the Buddha among Vishnu's *avatars*, but there he is, defined as the form under which Vishnu descended to earth to abolish blood sacrifice. Hinduism has unequalled powers of assimilation.

Shiva, the second of the main gods of Hinduism, came to assume a more ambiguous character as Vishnu. Dubbed the 'dreadful' and the 'ravisher' and described in terms that combine the attributes of Time and Death, he became the spirit of the underworld and cremation. As an ascetic of terrifying appearance, he is also the symbol of life, and is venerated in the temples in the form of the 'linga' or phallus. Under this aspect, he is Nataraja, the lord of the cosmic dance that by turn destroys worlds and creates them. A benevolent and redoubtable god, he is accompanied by the goddess Parvati, daughter of the god of mountains, Himavat (Himalayas). Shiva's mount is the bull Nandi, and his son is the elephant-headed god, Ganesha, the commander of the celestial army.

Certain Shivaite sects continue the blood sacrifices. But the development of Hinduism has increasingly tended to stress divine grace over sacrifice as the means to salvation. The new religion is based on *dharma*, the Law of the Universe, which is a

Page 14 above

The traditional image of Vishnu
More peaceful than the formidable Shiva, the god Vishnu is venerated throughout India in thousands of forms. One such is this little bronze statuette from southern India. With its typical attributes, it probably dates from the sixteenth century. (Musée d'Ethnographie, Geneva)

Architectural Monuments in Northern India

The geographical distribution of the Hindu temples presented here might lead to the impression that there were no such constructions in the north of the country, between Kashmir and the capital of Delhi. This imbalance, affecting the upper valley of the Indus and of the Satlej as well as the Yamuna Basin, is due to the catastrophic destruction that occurred in the wake of recurring Muslim invasions from the eleventh century onwards.

Nevertheless, in the north and north-west of India, important architectural developments also took place – for example, in early Gupta architecture (fourth and fifth centuries, in the area of the Ganges and Yamuna rivers) or in Rajput architecture (in the region of present-day Rajasthan). Once Muslim rule had spread over most of India, Hindu temple architecture only continued to evolve in the south of the subcontinent. Still, the fundamental influence exerted by northern India on the development of Hindu architecture should not be underestimated. While most of the sites and sanctuaries featured in this book are located in the Deccan, it must not be forgotten that Hindu art originated in the vast plain of the Ganges, where today only scant remains of its former florescence can be found.

moral law. It requires that humans attempt to become one with the universal soul and be restored to divinity, a goal attainable only after several cycles of reincarnation.

A Disconcerting Environment
This is the setting for our history of a tradition of religious architecture spanning more than a thousand years. The monuments to which it gave rise are many and varied, from the sanctuaries of isolated villages to the immense temple-cities of southern India and from the caves carved out of the rock with their mysterious hypostyle halls to the medieval temples with their towers covered in erotic or menacing sculptures. India is a world in itself. Its internal divisions have ebbed and flowed in the wake of its innumerable dynasties, and its indefinable history has left its civilisation focused on faith, ritual and theology.

Here then, at the edge of the jungle, by the crashing breakers of the ocean or in the silence of the rocky deserts in which the hermit and the *sadhu* perform their discipline of meditation, arise the Hindu temples that are the object of this study.

Page 14 below

A powerful sensuality
This torso of Parvati, Shiva's consort, expresses feminine beauty according to the canon of the south Indian sculptors. The eroticism is that of a young woman decorated with jewels, bracelets and necklaces. She wears an elaborate belt and the 'sacred cord' falls gracefully between her breasts. (Musée d'Ethnographie, Geneva)

THE FIRST ROCK-CUT TEMPLES

From Man-Made Caves to Stone-Built Temples

Page 17
Durga, the warrior-goddess with her bow
On the eastern shores of the Deccan, the monolithic temples (*rathas*) of Mamallapuram date from the seventh century. They are carved from a granite outcrop and imitate the forms of wood-framed architecture. The goddess Durga (the door-guard) is guarding the entrance of the Draupadi Ratha.

A panoramic low-relief at Mamallapuram
Detail from the great panel known as the 'Descent of the Ganges' or 'Arjuna's penance' (27 by 7 m) at Mamallapuram (seventh century). In the centre there is a little temple also in the Pallava style. In front of it gather ascetics, wild animals and celestial creatures. This vast work (page 35) is sculpted directly into the granite outcrop and represents Mount Kailasa, the Himalayan dwelling-place of Shiva.

The earliest works of Indian architecture are carved directly from the rock. Many of them are on a large scale and have survived nearly intact since they were built some fifteen or twenty centuries ago. Sacred man-made caves are a feature of both Brahmanic and Buddhist traditions. The forms are similar in both religions and testify to the origins of Indian architecture in primitive wooden buildings of which no traces now remain.

The rock-cut temples were hollowed out of mountains or seams carved out of hard stone and have more in common with sculpture than with conventional buildings constructed with blocks of dressed stone. Among these prototypical examples of Hindu architecture, we will look at the sites of Ellora, Elephanta and Mamallapuram, while at Udayagiri we find archaic caves carved by followers of Jain or Buddhist teachings.

There are two kinds of rock-cut architecture. The first is hollowed like an artificial cave out of a steep cliff and comprises vast chambers. The other is carved downwards into a rocky outcrop and creates architectural volumes of a sculptural character. The first kind consists of nothing but internal spaces; the second may altogether lack them. The caves of Elephanta and certain of the temples of Ellora are of the first kind, while the most famous of the second are the 'Seven Pagodas' or *rathas* sculpted out of the rock at Mamallapuram.

The gigantic Kailasa Temple at Ellora combines both kinds of rock-cut architecture. This monolithic building was carved out of the rock of a hillside, but its external shape, culminating in a pyramidal tower, rises directly into the open air, while its interior comprises several large hypostyle halls.

The Hindu builders, as these examples suggest, took the possibilities of rock-cut architecture to quite unexpected extremes. In doing so, they left fascinating evidence about the earliest Indian religious architecture.

For the great advantage of rock-cut architecture is its permanence. And the transition from the earlier wooden to stone buildings resulted in what could be described as a 'petrification' of forms; the heritage of the earliest periods was carefully transcribed into the new materials. This process on the one hand ensured formal continuity and on the other created a record of buildings whose organic materials – wood, thatch and palm-leaves – must soon have perished in India's humid climate.

The fact that the architectural features of these primitive temples were faithfully preserved in rock-cut sanctuaries can only be ascribed to the traditionalism and conservatism characteristic of religious thought. We shall take this process as our Ariadne's thread while describing the development of the earliest great sacred architecture in India.

Monolithic *rathas* at Mamallapuram

None of the monolithic temples carved from the Mamallapuram granite contains any internal spaces. They date from the seventh century and imitate in stone the earliest wooden temples. From right to left: Draupadi Ratha, dedicated to Durga; Arjuna Ratha, with its two-storeyed pyramidal roof; the Bhima Ratha, which imitates a Buddhist *chaitya*; and lastly another square temple but with a three-storeyed pyramidal roof, the Dharmaraja Ratha, which was built by King Narasimhavarman I between 630 and 660. In the foreground, Nandi the bull, Shiva's mount or 'vehicle'.

Architectural Sources

In the absence of archaeological evidence, it seems likely that no temples were
built in India during the Vedic age. The construction of rudimentary sacrificial altars
was in all likelihood as far as religious architecture went.

The forms of the earliest cave constructions can be traced back to secular architecture which still made use of perishable materials. The first transposition of this
formal language into stone was made in Buddhist and Jain edifices around the
second to first centuries B.C. The decisive factor for these developments was the
fact that Buddhism and Jainism were endorsed by rulers and rich merchants during
that period.

The history of Buddhist architecture will be the subject of a separate volume in
this series. Hindu architecture, however, cannot be understood without the knowledge gleaned from a study of the most ancient Buddhist monuments. They cast
considerable light on the birth of Brahmanic architecture. We shall therefore provide the basic information required in order to understand the origins of the Hindu
tradition.

The rise of Buddhism, which owed much to the support of the Emperor Ashoka,
found expression in the construction of three kinds of monument: the *stupa*, a kind
of emblematic mound, the *chaitya* or temple and the *vihara* or monastery. These
forms came to constitute the basic architectural language of India. For when the
first rock-cut edifices were constructed, from the third century B.C. on, they were
evidently informed by a pre-existing, and long-standing, tradition of wood-frame
building.

Buddhist Themes

Buddhist architecture was the first Indian tradition to find expression in durable buildings. Carved out of the living rock or built in carefully dressed stone, these buildings date from the third century B.C. They can be divided into the three categories required by the precepts of Buddha: temples, meeting-places and pilgrimage centres.

The sanctuaries (Sanskrit: *chaitya*) comprised a hall of basilican type with an apse containing a *stupa*. (The *stupa* was one of the few forms in which a symbolic representation of the Buddhist doctrine was permitted at this time.) The man-made caves that served as Buddhist temples generally possessed a sculpted façade. This reproduced the columns and decorative scheme of a wooden façade; at its centre was a wide bay whose vaulted opening was an extension of the barrel-vault of the hall. The features of a wooden roof-structure are reproduced in every detail.

The *vihara* or monastery was the second category of Buddhist building. There the inmates lived a life of meditation. A *vihara* normally originated as cave shelter; later there were integrated little rooms for religious cults. Carved out of the rock, *viharas* comprise a doorway leading on to a large courtyard with between one and three storeys of hypostyle halls and cells. There, the monks lived a communal existence. Monasteries were for those who had decided to give their life over to the precepts of the Enlightened One and to the rule of the monastic doctrine. There were monasteries for both sexes, though the sexes were always segregated in such communities.

Finally, the Buddha and his doctrine were commemorated in the form of *stupas*. These were funerary mounds of hemispherical shape, and a tradition of architecture developed around them. They had two functions: to mark the burial of sacred relics and to commemorate the main episodes of the Buddha's earthly mission. *Stupas* often became centres of pilgrimage, and were enriched with decorative elements, such as the *torana*, a kind of emblematic portal, and the *vedika*, a fence built in stone, which separated the ritual area from the surrounding secular space and defined the course of ritual circumambulation of the *stupa*.

The architectural heritage

When the first Hindu monuments were built, Buddhism had already created the *chaitya*, the *vihara* and the *stupa*.

Above left: the façade of a cave-temple *chaitya* at Ajanta, with its *chaitya*-arch window (sixth century).

Above right: the interior of a *chaitya*, with its carved stone imitation of a wooden barrel-vault (Ellora, early eighth century).

Centre left: the three-storeyed courtyard façade of a monastery or *vihara* at Ellora.

Centre right: the interior of a *vihara* at Ellora, with hypostyle hall and square pillars carved from the rock (eighth century).

Below: the great *stupa* at Sanchi, with the *vedika* enclosing it and one of the *toranas* or portals, dates from the first century B.C.

The Earliest Hindu Sanctuaries

Vernacular housing styles are the prototypes of the house of the god or gods. The divinity was originally housed in a little wooden hut roofed with thatch. So it seems likely that the 'petrification' phase was preceded by a long period in which perishable building materials were used. Then came a period of brick construction, during which sculptors were already working in stone. The first monuments built in dressed stone, such as the *stupa* at Sanchi, dates from the first century B.C.

Earlier than the first 'built' Buddhist monuments are the caves dug into the living rock by Buddhist builders at Lomas Rishi, Bhaja, Kondane and Ajanta. They date from the second and third centuries B.C. In them, we discern the prototypical wooden constructions they so faithfully imitate. Hindu and Buddhist builders alike borrowed the architectural and decorative forms of their rock-cut temples from wooden-framed buildings.

There is a reason why these Buddhist creations preceded their Hindu equivalents. The Emperor Ashoka promoted Buddhist doctrine and its expression in great buildings. At all events, there must have been a phase of Indian architecture of which nothing survives, a period in which only ephemeral materials were used and in which the architectural forms adopted by the different religions must have been very similar, since the forms of early Indian religious architecture all derive from vernacular housing.

Stone imitating wood at Mamallapuram
Detail of an engaged column at Mamallapuram. The intersecting brackets with their volute decorations clearly imitate wood-frame construction techniques.

The Temples of Mamallapuram

Founded by the Pallava dynasty which reigned over southern India between A.D. 566 and 894, the port city of Mamallapuram (also known as Mahabalipuram) features a series of buildings of supreme importance for the development of Hindu architecture. In addition to the famous 'Shore' Temple, to which we shall return, the site presents vast panoramic mythical scenes carved in low relief out of rocky outcrops as well as man-made caves serving as temples.

There is also a series of monolithic buildings carved out of the granite and preserving traces and forms of traditional vernacular housing. Forms of construction that had been developed for use with perishable materials were transformed to confer on the dwelling of the gods the 'eternal' quality of stone.

The *rathas* of Mamallapuram are not the earliest temples in non-perishable materials; but they are a good example of the process of petrification of form in Hindu architecture. They were carved in the mid-seventh century from an outcrop of pink granite and stand on what is now a sandy beach. Together, they form a composition remarkable for its variety of plans and elevations. The entire repertory of styles from south-east India has been 'tested' in these buildings and the *rathas* consequently display the full range of Hindu architectonic language. With extreme fidelity, they model forebears built with wooden frames and roofed with palm-leaves.

Principles and Analysis of Elements

The form of the *rathas* (which are as much sculptures as buildings) derives from simple principles. The sculptors, basing themselves on wood-frame architectural models, created an exterior imitating columns or pilasters; the capitals carry an entablature in which the ends of the crossbeams are clearly imitated.

The roof generally comprises a number of successive levels, each recessed relative to the one below. These form a step pyramid similar in effect to the corbelled roofs of later stone constructions built from the ground up. Hindu architecture, it should be noted at the outset, lacked all knowledge of the arch, vault and dome, for which false vaults made of criss-crossing roof-beams were substituted.

The decoration of the roof-storeys similarly affords considerable information concerning the perishable antecedents of this architecture. For emblematic reasons,

The dwelling of the gods
One of the miniature buildings that decorate the Dharmaraja Ratha at Mamallapuram (circa 630). We see the long side of a little house, in the centre of the roof a round window with wide frame (*kudu*). Below, the *kudu* theme is repeated, with a head appearing at the window to show the houses are inhabited. They represent the home of the gods on Mount Kailasa.

Page 24 below
Sculpted from the Mamallapuram granite
Just as the architectural forms of the Mamallapuram *rathas* are sculpted in the living granite, so too are the ornamental sculptures that adorn these 'buildings'. At the Arjuna Ratha, built in the seventh century, Shiva, Durga and another graceful couple flank the central sculpture of Shiva at the south wall.

the *rathas* are ornamented with small-scale models of huts arranged around the entire perimeter of the roof ('square' *stupis* and oblong *shalas*). And each of these miniature huts has its own barrel-vaulted roof, its palm or straw roof carefully depicted in stone. The section of the barrel-vault forms at the end an opening that also served as a window. This tympanum-like motif is highly significant; it is known as the *kudu* or *chaitya* arch.

Now these features clearly define a *chaitya* façade, reproducing on a much-reduced scale the kind of cave entrance façades found at Ajanta, Lomas Rishi, Karle and Ellora. In many cases, the *kudu* is ornamented with little sculpted figures who appear to be looking out of the arched window. Their heads emerge at the centre of the bay, as if to contemplate the world outside.

The *Kudu* – An Omnipresent Symbol

The *kudu* came to play an important symbolic role in Indian architecture of both Buddhist and Hindu inspiration.

The rows of miniaturised buildings on the successive roof-levels of sacred buildings are pregnant with symbolism: they form an image of the celestial city. They represent at times the dwelling of Shiva, on the summit of the Himalayan peak Mount Kailasa, and at times Mount Meru, the mythical mountain of Indian cosmology, which was considered the axis of the world and the meeting-place of the gods. At the summit lived Brahma, the creator of the universe. Brahma, in combination with Vishnu and Shiva, constituted the *trimurti* or triumvirate of gods who reigned over creation, preservation and destruction.

This representation of the world of the gods crowning the Hindu temple conferred on the building a very particular sanctity. In short, the recurrent symbol of the mythical summit of the world, Kailasa, of which many examples will be found in this study, can legitimately be regarded as a *leitmotif* of Hindu architecture. The *kudu* motif can, moreover, be used to evoke Kailasa on its own, without the *stupi* and *shala* aedicules on which it often appears.

At the summit of several *rathas* stands a hemispherical or octagonal *stupi*, which is also decorated with *kudu* motifs. This would seem to be a symbol of the celestial dome that covers the dwelling of the gods.

Mount Meru at Mamallapuram
Crowned by an octagonal
monolithic 'dome' (stupi), the
Arjuna Ratha at Mamallapuram
(seventh century) is seen here
with its western façade sunlit.
Its early pyramidal roof has only
two storeys and is decorated with
miniature buildings representing
the world of the gods on the
cosmic mountain (Mount Meru
or Mount Kailasa).

**Symbolic architecture at
Mamallapuram**
The entrance gallery of the
monolithic Arjuna Ratha at
Mamallapuram is a dead end;
the centre of the temple is
solid. On the roof can be seen
the little huts that represent
the city of the gods.

Varieties of *Ratha*

The smallest of the Mamallapuram *rathas*, known as the Draupadi Ratha, is dedicated to the goddess Durga. Square in plan, its roof is a projecting curvilinear structure of four planes, like that of a hut roofed with palm-leaves.

When monolithic buildings were replaced by constructions of dressed stone,
this type of roof proved too difficult to build and was abandoned. Note that the
corner ridges are decorated with delicate carvings; their volutes stand out above
niches containing high-relief carvings of the goddess to whom the *ratha* is dedicated, Durga. On either side of this monolith are two great free-standing images:
a lion and a Nandi bull.

The second *ratha*, that of Arjuna, is a fine example of the step-pyramid structure decorated with miniature buildings. The latter are oblong along the sides
(*shalis*) and square at the corners (*stupis*) and they imitate the successive levels of the
cosmic mountain. The Arjuna Ratha is of square plan and modest dimensions, its
sides being only 5 m long. The high-relief sculptures on the external walls are
set between pilasters of a kind that, in the wooden original, would have supported the roof. The sculptures show the god Shiva along with Vishnu and tower
guardians.

The third *ratha*, called the Bhima Ratha, reproduces the *chaitya* model. It is
sculpted in the image of the halls that were used as Buddhist meeting-places. We
know what the interiors of these halls looked like from the faithful record offered
by the Buddhist cave-temples. The roof of the Bhima Ratha is in barrel-vault style,

The Bhima Ratha at Mamallapuram
Elevation of the Bhima Ratha at Mamallapuram (seventh century). The entrance portico has four free-standing columns and a series of *kudus* running along the entablature. Above them are the miniature buildings found on all four sides of the temple. A saddle-back roof with concave sides and dormer windows runs the full length of the building.

A Hindu shrine following a Buddhist model

The design of the Bhima Ratha is based on one of the fundamental forms of Indian architecture: the elongated meeting hall. This con- struction type, which is often bordered by rows of columns and topped by a cylindrical roof, also served as model for the Buddhist *chaitya* halls (although the latter are found as cave constructions within natural openings in the rock, whereas the Bhima Ratha was carved out of a rock wall itself). Furthermore, as opposed to the Buddhist cave constructions, the apsidal rear end is missing here.

Above left

Building within a building at Mamallapuram

A miniature temple of the kind that we have seen in the 'Descent of the Ganges' (page 18) occupies the tympanum of the Bhima Ratha dating from the seventh century. The monolithic *ratha* is decorated with a little temple of its own, to indicate its sacred function.

Above right

The façade of a divine palace in Mamallapuram

The long façade of the Bhima Ratha seems to reproduce that of a primitive palace, here representing the residence of the gods.

Lions guard the Bhima Ratha at Mamallapuram

The columns of the Bhima Ratha at Mamallapuram rise from the heads of seated lions. At Kanchipuram, the dressed stone Pallava temples exhibit similar columns rising from rampant lions.

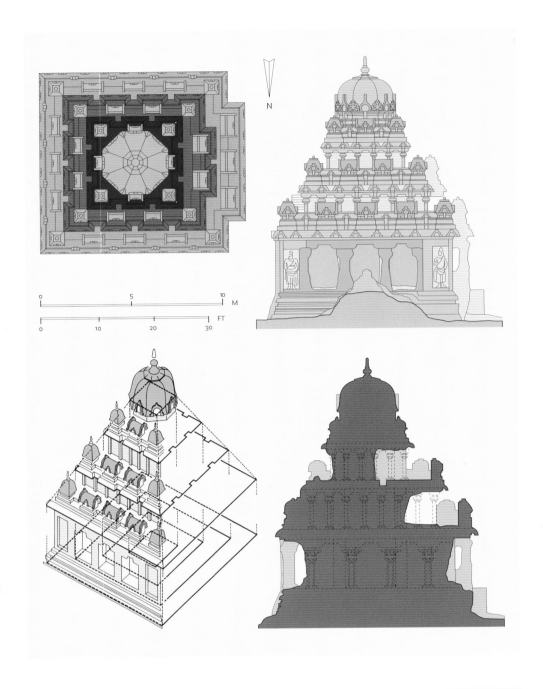

The Dharmaraja Ratha at Mamallapuram
Plan of the roof-storeys, eleva-tion, axonometric drawing and section of the Dharmaraja or Yuddhishthira Ratha at Mamalla-puram that was founded about 630 by King Narasimhavarman I. Its roof-storeys are ornamented with some forty miniature build-ings representing the dwellings of Shiva and other gods on the cosmic mountain (Mount Kailasa).

Below
The emblematic architecture of Mamallapuram
The west façade of the Dharma-raja or Yuddhishthira Ratha at Mamallapuram. This monolithic sanctuary is dedicated to Shiva and faithfully translates the symbolic structure of the wooden temples that preceded stone architecture in the Hindu tradition.

Page 31
Transposition into stone at Mamallapuram
Western façade of the Dharmaraja or Yuddhishthira Ratha at Mamal-lapuram.

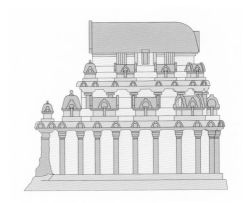

The Buddhist tradition reflected at Mamallapuram
Façade (left) and apse (right) of the Nakula Sahadeva Ratha at Mamallapuram dating from the seventh century. Its apsidal form derives from the semicircular terminations of Buddhist *chaityas*, in which a *stupa* was so placed that the rite of circumambulation could be observed.

and can, unlike the cave-temple roofs, be seen from the outside; the short sides of the roof present the form of the *kudu*, the end-section of the barrel-vault. On the long sides of the building are columns carved from the rock that resemble those running along the sides of the rock-cut *chaitya* halls at Ellora and Ajanta. At Mamallapuram, the bases of these columns are in the form of seated lions; the columns grow out of the lions' heads. Along the cornices apparently supporting the roof run miniature edifices and *kudu*-form bays. The only point on which the Bhima Ratha differs from a *chaitya* is the absence of an apsidal end. The main entrance is on one of the long sides.

The fourth *ratha*, the Dharmaraja or Yuddhishthira Ratha, was built by King Narasimhavarman I, who reigned from circa 630. Dedicated to Shiva, it is the largest of the five *rathas*. It is square in plan, with sides about 10 m long. The third level of its pyramidal roof is 13 m high. Essentially monolithic, the Ratha has no internal spaces other than the galleries with carved columns at the entrance and apsidal ends. Overall, it is a larger-scale version of the Arjuna Ratha, but with one further roof-storey and a larger number of miniature edifices carved into the roof. There are twelve

The royal lion at Mamallapuram
Detail of a 'heraldic' lion ornamenting a pier of the Ganesha Ratha at Mamallapuram, which was formerly dedicated to Shiva (left). The same motif is found at the base of the columns of this little monolithic sanctuary (right). The roof has two storeys of miniature buildings.

Page 32 below
The influence of the *chaitya* at Mamallapuram
Side elevation of the Nakula Sahadeva Ratha at Mamallapuram. Its roof 'vault' is inspired by the barrel-vaults of wooden Buddhist temples.

square *stupis* at the corners and twenty-four *shalas* on the sides, all of them exhibiting the *kudu* motif.

The fifth *ratha* at Mamallapuram, the Nakula Sahadeva Ratha, reproduces the basilican plan with apsidal end and barrel-vault characteristic of the Buddhist *chaitya*.

In the seventh-century monuments of Mamallapuram, then, we see the entire formal repertory of an architecture used and developed by both the Hindu and Buddhist religions and their religious duties.

There are other *rathas* at Mamallapuram, such as the Ganesha Ratha, in addition to cave-temples such as the Mandapa (dance hall) of Krishna, also called the Tiger (Yali) Cave, and the great relief sculpture called the 'Descent of the Ganges' or 'Arjuna's Penance'.

A pavilion for ritual dance at Mamallapuram
The entrance portico of a man-made cave at Mamallapuram. Behind the *mandapa*, the entrance hall, the sanctum lies deep in the rock. The columns rising from seated lions are typical of the Pallava style.

The Tiger Cave at Mamallapuram
Outside the present-day city of Mamallapuram is a man-made cave excavated from the granite that has at its centre the façade of a small temple. It is preceded by steps and flanked by two columns in the form of rampant tigers. The grinning muzzles of enormous tigers surround the entrance to the cave, which lies close to the shore.

Praying to Shiva at Mamallapuram
The great relief panel of the
'Descent of the Ganges'. In the
centre of historical Mamallapuram, this huge, unfinished sculpture, with its dozens of figures,
celestial beings and animals, constitutes a monumental Shivaite
scene. We see the King Ayudhya as
an ascetic petitioning Shiva to let
the power of the river Ganges flow
in such a way, that the cosmos
would not be damaged. The 'river
bed' is seen as deep notch in the
centre of the rock where *nagas*
(snake-beings) haloed in cobra-
heads move upwards. Every living
thing awaits the beneficent
waters of the Ganges. In the centre there is a little temple before
which other ascetics are praying
(see detail on page 18). The work
dates from the mid-seventh century.

**Power and majesty in the
'Descent of the Ganges'**
One of the majestic elephants
depicted standing on the banks of
the sacred river as they await the
flow of waters petitioned from
Shiva. The quality of this sculpture
is eloquent witness to Indian
familiarity with an animal
frequently found working alongside man. Ganesha, the son of
Shiva and Parvati, is the god of
wisdom and is symbolised by the
elephant.

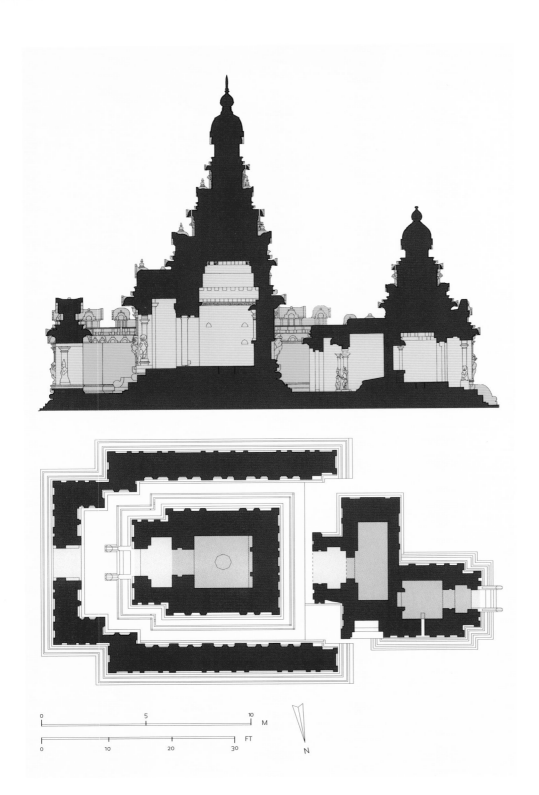

The Shore Temple at Mamallapuram
Longitudinal section and plan of the temple, which was built about 700. The temple comprises three shrines, or *shikharas*, the more important square one dedicated to Shiva and the smaller rectangular one to Vishnu. The main building stands in a precinct, within which there is a circumambulatory passage.

The Transition to Stone-Built Architecture

Looking out over the Mamallapuram shoreline
The Shore Temple at Mamallapuram was built by Nrisimhavarman II Rajasimha on a promontory that juts out into the ocean in the early eighth century. Unlike the monolithic *rathas*, it is made of finely dressed blocks of local granite.

Based on a symbolic scheme like that of the square *rathas*, the Shore Temple at Mamallapuram, constructed about 700 by Nrisimhavarman II Rajasimha (circa A.D. 700–728), is a transposition of the formula of the monolithic temples, but this time constructed in carefully dressed blocks of granite. Its slender tower rises 16 m above the beach and the rectangular temple compound. The building is oriented east, towards the ocean. Though the temple is dedicated to Shiva, as the numerous statues of the bull Nandi on the compound wall indicate, behind it is a secondary temple with a statue of Vishnu. A third smaller temple contains a *linga* too and opens towards the west.

The two towers of the temple present the now classical ornamentation of miniature buildings. The regular courses of immaculately dressed granite made it possible to infuse this ornamental scheme with greater vigour and autonomy; the miniature buildings are each of them an independent unit, and behind them runs a dwarf gallery. The soaring verticality of the Shore Temple's elevation is accentuated by the relatively slender monolithic *stupi* crowning the tower. This verticality is, as we shall see, a characteristic perpetuated in the Hindu architectural tradition as a whole.

Though eroded by the salt spray, the Shore Temple is one of the great successes of an art that had already attained maturity. And it has an admirable setting, though this has been somewhat altered by the drastic 'salvage' work undertaken recently under the auspices of UNESCO in order to distance the temple from the sea-swell washing at its foundations.

The slender towers of the Shore Temple
Standing one behind the other, the towers of the Shore Temple at Mamallapuram (circa 700) resemble the *rathas* in having stepped roof-storeys decorated with miniature buildings and culminating in monolithic octagonal domes. In the foreground, eroded Nandi bull sculptures.

The Shore Temple's lofty silhouette
The walls of the Shore Temple precinct are lined with sculptures of the bull Nandi. To the left, we see the smaller, to the right the higher *shikhara* of the Shore Temple. The miniature buildings lining the stepped roof-storeys symbolise Kailasa, the cosmic mountain, home of the gods.

Kanchipuram

Kanchipuram is one of the holy cities of Hinduism. It was the capital of the Pallava dynasty, which reigned over southern India in the seventh and eighth centuries.

Here stands the great Kailasanatha Temple, a remarkable example of a temple constructed, like the Shore Temple at Mamallapuram, from the ground up by Nrisimhavarman II Rajasimha. Built between 700 and 728, it is in a remarkable state of preservation. It is dedicated to Shiva and its name, the Kailasanatha, immediately places it in the tradition of temples celebrating the cosmic mountain. It does indeed possess a sturdy pyramidal tower, flanked on all four sides by small shrines. The tower or *shikhara* comprises four stepped storeys ornamented, like the temples of Mamallapuram, with a multitude of miniature buildings.

Under the tower is a cella in which the linga of the god is presented. A modern hypostyle hall today links the tower to a *mandapa* or dancing hall, which was formerly free-standing. The temple as a whole is oriented eastwards, and stands within a large courtyard preceded by a gateway or *gopuram*, which is of modest dimensions compared with later developments.

The courtyard walls are lined inside with little shrines; ritual circumambulation thus takes place between these shrines and the sanctuary itself. Other shrines stand outside the entrance to the sanctuary, so that there is a total of fifty-five such small shrines. Each of them is covered with an octagonal dome, on top of which stands a *stupi*. The shrines have a role similar to that of the miniature edifices that decorate the towers of Pallava-style buildings.

The interest of this fine eighth-century temple is that it provides an almost intact example of the organisation of a Shivaite sanctuary. The quality of the

The Kailasanatha Temple at Kanchipuram
The precinct of the Kailasanatha Temple with its many shrines is visible behind a large ablution tank lined with steps. To the left is the *gopuram*, or portal, and, to the right, the imposing main shrine.

Page 41 below left
Plan of the Kailasanatha Temple at Kanchipuram
The plan of the Kailasanatha Temple shows the layout of a typical Pallava sanctuary. Behind a row of shrines (below), the entrance leads through a smaller shrine to the courtyard. An open corridor flanked with shrines surrounds the temple, which comprises two hypostyle *mandapas*. Through them one reaches the cella in which stands Shiva's symbol, the linga. Around the square *garbha griha* (main shrine) is a narrow circumambulatory passage.

The hypostyle pavilion of the Kailasanatha Temple

In front of the tower of the Kailasanatha Temple at Kanchipuram is the hypostyle pavilion (*mandapa*) decorated with sculptures in which emblematic lions alternate with sculpted divinities. The first hypostyle hall leads through to a second and thence to the *garbha griha*. This, in its turn, is contained within a narrow corridor and has seven shrines on its external walls.

Below right

The outer corridor of the Kailasanatha Temple

The Kailasanatha Temple at Kanchipuram was constructed by King Narasimharvan II. It features an open-air 'ambulatory' lined by fifty-two shrines. Pillars and columns rise from the heads of rampant lions in typical Pallava style.

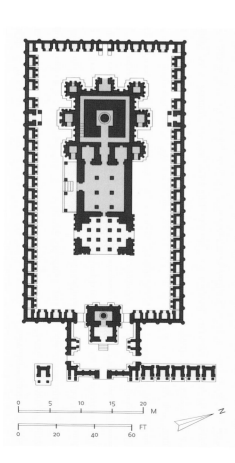

sculpture and, in particular, of the columns set on rearing lions, makes the Kaila-sanatha Temple a perfect example of south Indian Hindu art.

Of similar kind, but less well preserved, is the Venkanatha or Vaikuntha Perumal Temple, which dates from circa 750 and is consecrated to Vishnu. Its three-level tower is some 20 m high and is similarly adorned with miniature buildings. The cella, which houses a statue of Vishnu, is preceded by a *mandapa* with two bays of four columns. The building as a whole is surrounded by a gallery, whose columns rise from the heads of rearing lions. This colonnade leaves too narrow a space for the spectator to be able to stand back from the building and contemplate the tower. It was intended to guide the processions of the faithful in their circumambulations. The walls of the gallery are covered in reliefs that illustrate the legendary battles betweeen the Pallavas and their neighbours the Chalukyas, whose dynasty reigned from about 500 to 888.

Kanchipuram shows Pallava art finding its fullest expression in temples constructed from regular courses using carefully dressed stone, often without any form of mortar. The temples and precincts are ornamented on the one hand with sculptures and reliefs representing mythical scenes and the struggles of the Pallava dynasty, on the other with miniature buildings symbolising, here as elsewhere, the residence of the gods on the sacred mountain.

The glory of Shiva in the Kailasanatha Temple
With its projecting shrines surrounding the cella, its pillars rising from rampant lions and the sculptures of the bull Nandi, the Kailasanatha Temple at Kanchipuram, built circa 720, is a perfect example of Dravidian architecture.

Vishnu honoured at Kanchipuram
In the Pallava capital, the less well preserved Vaikuntha Perumal, or Venkanatha Temple is dedicated to Vishnu and was built after 750. It has a classic stepped *shikhara*.

The Venkanatha Temple's circumambulatory corridor
The portico that surrounds the Venkanatha Temple in Kanchipuram. The temple was built on a smaller scale than the Kailasanatha Temple and its corridor is so narrow that the tower can scarcely be seen by the devotee.

The Rock-Cut Temple at Elephanta

About 1000 km north-west of Kanchipuram lies Elephanta, one of the greatest achievements of rock-cut architecture. Here Brahmanic art and architecture attain a level bordering on perfection.

Not far from the modern city of Bombay, which became a powerful industrial city under the influence of the British Raj during the nineteenth century, Elephanta is a small island whose serenity lends itself to religious meditation. The rock-cut temple, which is dedicated to Shiva, was created in the mid-sixth century and is enormous. The sanctuary forms a complex of chambers cut from the rock, with one main and two lateral portals, a cruciform hypostyle hall flanked by external courtyards, and various smaller chambers of worship. The overall size of the complex is 80 m by 80 m.

Page 44

The rock-cut columns of Elephanta

The great hypostyle hall of the rock-cut temple at Elephanta (sixth century), near Bombay, is a man-made cave. Its ceiling rests on twenty pillars, whose square shafts are surmounted by fluted cylindrical columns. The sturdy circular cushion capitals are also fluted. The majesty of these supports testifies to a Hindu cave architecture that dates back to the eighth century.

The colossal *trimurti* image at Elephanta

The three-headed colossus at Elephanta represents the god Shiva. Its high tiaras are shadowed by the penumbral atmosphere of the cave-temple. The meditative concentration and other-worldly serenity of its faces mark out this sixth-century work as one of the masterpieces of Hindu art.

Plan of Elephanta

The rock-cut sanctuary of Elephanta is very precisely oriented. At its centre is a hypostyle hall of 20 pillars, in which stands the cruciform cella containing Shiva's image, the linga. To the east of the central cave-temple, a courtyard precedes a second temple; to the west, there is a smaller and darker courtyard.

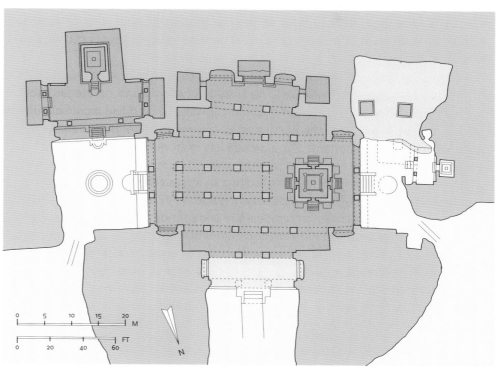

The most impressive element in this vast shadowy space is the twenty-pillared
hall containing the square cella in which the linga of the god is venerated. Along the
axis of the temple, though at right angles to the north portal, two rows of four
columns form a nave that serves as the *mandapa*, the space given over to music and
dance.

The hall thus contains an oblong space offering those who come to meditate the
protection of its forest of columns. The fluted columns stand on elegant square
bases and are crowned with fluted cushion capitals. Behind the *mandapa*, illumi-
nated by the diffuse light of the north portal, emerges the enigmatic image of the
sadashiva, the manifest form of Shiva, which lies in front of the northern entrance
and represents a contrast to the linga, the symbolic form of Shiva.

This architectural complex was created by carving out the living rock, from which
the statues, columns and internal spaces are made. The construction took place, as
it were, in reverse, by a process of removal and elimination, where normally an architect would think in terms of addition and augmentation. So the entire temple can
be compared to a huge sculpture through which the visitor walks, discovering lateral chambers, cells and sinuous corridors. A balance is consciously maintained
between areas of untreated bare rock and surfaces wrought to a high polish. The art
of Elephanta thus contrasts with Nature its own refined aesthetic, whose subtlety
is directed towards heightening a 'pantheistic' religious experience.

The Caves at Ellora

Ellora, not far from present-day Aurangabad, is less than 300 km from Bombay. This famous place was the site of an extraordinary artistic flowering, in which Buddhist, Hindu and Jain art all participated. More than thirty temples have been carved out of the cliff-face or sculpted from the hillside. They form an ensemble of an unique kind, dating between the sixth and the ninth centuries, though activity was most intense under the Rashtrakuta dynasty (754–982). Beyond the intrinsic value of many of the monuments of Ellora, their association with each other – bringing together as it does the three great religions derived from Vedic beliefs – represents a moving example of Indian religious feeling.

We pass over the Buddhist southern group, caves 1–12; these superb *chaityas* and *viharas* will be dealt with in a separate volume in this series. In what follows, we confine ourselves to the main Jain and Hindu caves, sizeable internal spaces specifically designed as religious architecture.

First in order is the elegant façade of Cave 21, known as the Rameshvara. It dates from the late sixth century and is dedicated to the cult of Shiva. Both sides of the veranda show river goddesses. Notable among these is the graceful Ganga (the Ganges), treading underfoot the *makara*, a sort of monster combining elements of the crocodile, dolphin and elephant. Other deities are visible on the façade and on the richly decorated capitals of columns that rise out of low walls. Their delicate presence is also found in the form of brackets, which, unlike those in dressed-stone temples, here form part of the solid mass of rock from which the columns were cut. The cave opens on to a large, oblong chamber (with two further rooms or recesses at either side), which leads into the sanctuary itself. Its cella contains a linga and is surrounded by a corridor for circumambulation.

Other caverns are much larger again. The Dhumar Lena, Cave 29, is one such. It is cruciform in plan and contains a hypostyle hall whose columns have square bases and are crowned by fluted cushion capitals of bulbous form. The hall is reached via staircases that lead up to the entrance gallery, which is flanked on either side by

Plan of the Rameshvara Cave at Ellora

In front of Cave 21 at Ellora is a great square courtyard, whose entrance portico consists of finely carved columns rising from low walls. Behind the portico is an oblong hall with, left and right, a small shrine and, straight ahead, the square cella, which lies within a circumambulatory corridor and is, like the two small shrines, preceded by two columns.

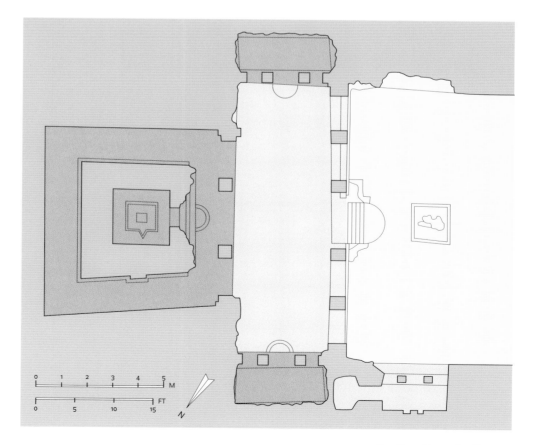

A vast hypostyle hall at Ellora
Preceded by columns such
as those at Elephanta the cruciform hall of Cave 29 at Ellora is
thought to date from the mid-seventh century. This rock-cut work,
known as the Dhumar Lena or
Sitaki-Nahani Cave (Sita's Bath),
has at its centre a square *garbha
griha*. The pairs of *dvarapalas*
mount guard over the *linga*.

Page 48
River goddesses at Ellora
A detail of the sculpted façade
of the Rameshvara Cave, built
at the end of the sixth century.
The goddess Ganga takes up
her elegant stance on a mythical
river monster, the *makara*.

densely carved mythological scenes in which the awesome Shiva has a prominent
place. In the centre is the quadrilateral cella, open on all four sides to allow sight of
the linga, the emblem of the divinity. This 'holy of holies' occupies the middle of the
composition, thus allowing the devotees simultaneously to perform the ritual of
circumambulation. The walls of the Dhumar Lena Cave are covered in high-relief
statues to the glory of Shiva, who is represented in various episodes from his
legends, in particular those in which he is paired with his wife Parvati.

When one considers not only the immense quantities of rock excavated to create
these temples but also the quality of the sculptures carved direct into the rock, one
is overwhelmed with admiration. The precision of the carving and the authority of
the sculptors who created these sacred scenes with their powerful symbolism are
astounding.

In these works, Hindu rock-cut art of the sixth, seventh and eighth centuries
attains its classical phase if not its culmination.

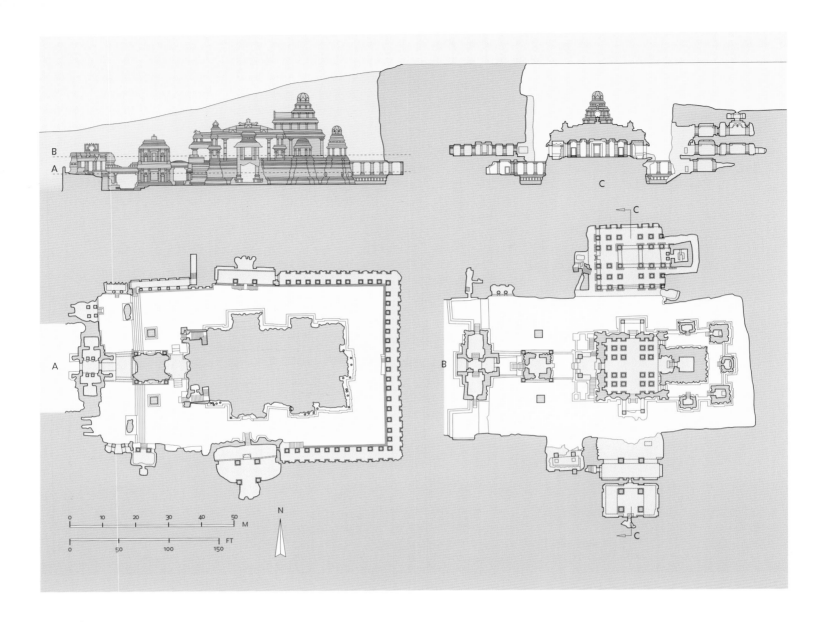

| 0 | 10 | 20 | 30 | 40 | 50 |
M
| 0 | | 50 | | 100 | | 150 |
FT

N

The Kailasa Temple at Ellora

Nevertheless, Cave 16, the Kailasa Temple, is undoubtedly the most sublime monument at Ellora. Unlike the caves tunnelled into the cliff, whose façades alone are visible from outside and whose internal spaces are chambers within the hillside, the Kailasa Temple is a gigantic monolithic temple, its ornate exterior open to the air like a sculpture of architectural dimensions.

In aspect it is a typical Dravidian temple, comprising gateway (*gopuram*), courtyard, aedicule for the bull Nandi, the mount of Shiva, large hypostyle *mandapa*, and an imposing tower (*shikhara*). The tower is conventionally composed of successively receding storeys decorated with miniature buildings symbolising the celestial world.

One should also note what is perhaps the most astonishing feature of the complex, the deep narrow passage that surrounds the temple. This forms a colonnaded gallery running along the bottom of the vertiginous cliff face. Lateral sanctuaries at first- and second-storey levels offer vast hypostyle interiors in the manner of cave-temples.

The Kailasa Temple is dedicated to Shiva. Built in the reign of Dantidurga and Krishna I, between 757 and 773, it is the largest monolithic temple in India, being 100 m long and 75 m wide. It is dominated by the enormous square-plan tower, which symbolises the cosmic mountain and reaches a height of 30 m.

The rock-cut Kailasa Temple
The largest rock-cut work at Ellora is Temple 16. Dating from 757–773, it represents the sacred mountain of Shiva. The plans give some idea of the sheer size of this temple, which was carved from the rock in its entirety: clockwise – longitudinal section; cross-section; ground floor plan; first storey.

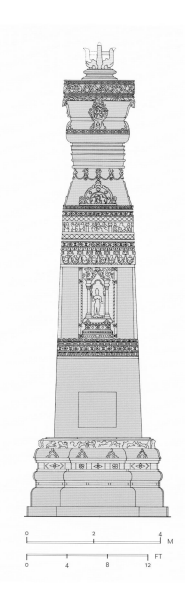

0   2   4   M

0   4   8   12   FT

The 'obelisks' at Ellora
On either side of the main temple
of the Kailasa complex stand 16 m
high pillars decorated with relief
carvings.

Emblematic monuments at Ellora
Inspired by columns built in front
of temples, these monumental
pillars, were made – like the entire
Kailasa complex – by excavation
not construction.

Virtuoso excavation work at the Kailasa Temple
Entirely carved out of the mountainside, the Kailasa Temple at Ellora is a version of the style of temple established by the Pallava dynasty in southern India. But the dressed-stone Pallava temples were considerably smaller than their monolithic equivalent. In the foreground, we see the tall *shikhara* and behind it the *mandapa*; to the right is the entrance *gopuram* or portal.

Page 53
The monumental tower of the Kailasa Temple
The tower of the Kailasa Temple (built between 757 and 773) soars upwards in imitation of the mountainous dwelling of Shiva. Each of its storeys is decorated with miniature buildings to represent the homes of the gods and the *stupi* at the summit follows the precedent set by the *rathas* at Mamallapuram. Around the temple stand four sculpted bulls representing Nandi, Shiva's 'vehicle'.

The sculpting of this monument required the removal of some 400 000 tonnes of rock. In the Kailasa Temple, the order of events recorded at Mamallapuram has been reversed. There, as we saw, the *rathas* were carved from the rock while the later Shore Temple was built in dressed stone. The temple at Ellora is exactly contemporary with the Shore Temple, but the excavation–sculpture method was nonetheless preferred. This is paradoxical, for in drawing up his plans the architect of the Kailasa Temple was clearly inspired by south-east Indian dressed-stone temples, such as those of Mamallapuram and Kanchipuram. But his own realisation of their plans took monolithic form, again through a kind of petrification. The architectural elements of dressed-stone temples have all been reproduced, and the forms of the Kailasa's models have been reproduced in every detail, despite the very different techniques required. The comparison with Mamallapuram, and even with Kanchipuram, is relevant not least because we know that Krishna I sought architects from the Pallava kingdom for the construction of the Kailasa Temple. The Pallava temples were chosen as models and then influenced the design of the Kailasa Temple.

But the architect also made ingenious and original use of the technique of rock-cutting. In the courtyard behind the *gopuram*, on either side of the little temple consecrated to Nandi the bull that precedes the temple proper, he provided for two obelisk-like pillars. Standing 16 m high, they are 'adaptations' of the Ashoka pillars. Similar votive or emblematic pillars are found in many Buddhist but also Hindu monuments. But there is no evidence for the existence of such pillars in the models on which the Kailasa Temple drew – though it is of course possible that non-monolithic pillars existed but, proving less durable, have not survived.

Carving the temple from the hillside required whole armies of workers. They created the forms of the sanctuary by gradually cutting down from above. Probably

The cliff face surrounding the Kailasa Temple
The space that encircles the Kailasa Temple at Ellora is cut directly from the rock. On either side of the temple are further rock-cut spaces within the cliff face; here, on the north side, they comprise two storeys of hypostyle halls and porticoed galleries. The space between temple and cliff provides for the ritual of circumambulation.

Sculpture and excavation: the Kailasa Temple

Treated as sculpture in the round, then excavated to form interiors, this square pavilion (Nandi *mandapa*) faces the *mandapa* proper on the first storey. It imitates the little pavilions found in medieval Indian architecture, in particular those at Pattadakal (page 79).

The hypostyle pavilion of the Kailasa

An enormous hypostyle hall precedes the sanctum of the Kailasa Temple at Ellora. In this *mandapa*, the sacred ballet of Shiva Nataraja, the Lord of the Cosmic Dance, received the homage of Hindu ritual, preparing the faithful for contact with the god in the sanctum.

Remnants of colour on the Kailasa Temple

The entire Kailasa complex at Ellora (built between 757 and 773) was not merely sculpted but probably already at that time stuccoed and painted in vibrant colours as well. Today, only vestiges of this treatment remain to give us an idea of its original appearance, painted all over in bright red, green and blue on a white background. The relief scenes with their Shivaite iconography are framed by architectural structures in which we recognise the signs of wood-frame architecture transposed into stone: pilasters, capitals, corbels and so on.

they first cut the deep trenches of the corridor surrounding the temple, leaving the central block intact. Then they dug out the gallery and the lateral chambers, developing a technique for removing the vast quantities of rock they dislodged by channelling down into the valley.

Only then did the sculptors themselves intervene. It was they who gave life to this proliferation of monsters, fabulous animals, guardian elephants, lions, divinities, mythical scenes and the repeated motifs of the omnipresent ornamentation. Everything is meticulously sculpted from the rock and there is no trace of alterations or second thoughts.

But this impeccable execution underlay a further, surprising aspect of the Kailasa Temple: its stone was next stuccoed over and painted in bright colours. Vestiges of this technique can still be seen under the overhang of the roof. In contrast with the black granite that greets one today, the Kailasa Temple was painted white all over, with dashes of exuberant red, blue and yellow.

These polychrome remains make it clear that the gaudy *gopurams* of southern India are in direct line of descent from a millennarian tradition. The visitor is inclined to think that the riot of colour characterising the sixteenth and seventeenth centuries is a later phenomenon in which the Brahmanic temple undergoes a conversion to the baroque. The Kailasa Temple clearly demonstrates the contrary.

But there is more to the Kailasa Temple than its sculpted, stuccoed and painted exterior. It also possesses remarkable interior spaces, painstakingly excavated from the rock. The workers were careful to retain pillars 'supporting' the roof, as in a dressed-stone temple, both in the central hypostyle hall and in the several floors of sanctuaries on either side of it. This excavated architecture creates impressively large interiors. The central *mandapa* measures 18 m² and has sixteen square pillars. At 20 by 25 m (500 m²) the northern sanctuary is larger still and has thirty admirably wrought pillars.

A Jain sanctuary at Ellora
Cave 32 at Ellora, the Indra Sabha
Temple, dates from the ninth to
tenth centuries. Like the Kailasa
Temple, though on a much smaller
scale, it has an open courtyard. In
it stands this fine elephant,
sculpted in the round.

**The Ashoka-column theme at
the Indra Sabha Temple**
This column at the Indra Sabha
Temple at Ellora is, like the
'obelisks' of the Kailasa Temple,
the equivalent of traditional pillars in front of Hindu temples.
Like them, it was created by
excavation. A little pavilion
greets the visitor.

Mahavira in the Indra
Sabha Temple
At the back of the hypostyle hall
of the Jain Indra Sabha Temple at
Ellora, high-relief panels depict
episodes in the life of Mahavira,
called Jina, the Victorious, and his
twenty-three predecessors.

The Jain Caves at Ellora

We could hardly write of Ellora without referring to the beautiful Jain Caves and
rock-cut architecture to be found to the north of the site. The most remarkable of
them is the Indra Sabha Temple (Cave 32). It dates from the ninth or tenth centuries.
Like the Kailasa Temple, it is partly open to the air. Its central structure is a pyramidal tower rising over a cella. In the courtyard a free-standing elephant and column
declare the thematic elements the cave shares with the Kailasa Temple, though they
appear here on a much smaller scale.

It is the internal spaces of the Indra Sabha Temple that constitute its main attraction, in particular the upper chamber, a superlative hypostyle hall. Carved from the
rock, its splendid columns are set on square bases, while their cylindrical upper
parts terminate in capitals bearing a series of fluted rings. The prolific ornament
and elegant proportions of the hall are the great merits of this form of architecture. On the walls are sculpted panels in a dense, rich style perfectly at one with
the ornament, relating episodes from the life of Jina. The hagiographical figures
are accompanied by garlands of flowers and vine branches. Throughout the cave,
the sculptors demonstrated prodigious mastery.

Page 59
**Rock-cut rococo in the Indra
Sabha Temple**
The colonnaded hypostyle hall
on two sides of the Indra Sabha
Temple exhibits curious columns.
The fluted shaft stands on a
moulded square base and is
decorated with a cubic band
richly carved with volutes and
arabesques. The cushion capital
is also fluted and supports a large
rectangular abacus.

THE GREAT FLOWERING OF MEDIEVAL TEMPLES

From the Chalukya School to the Cholas of Thanjavur

In our descriptions of Mamallapuram, Elephanta and Ellora, we saw that the Hindu temple consisted of certain essential components and conformed to certain fundamental rules. The sanctum containing the statue or symbol of the divinity (for example, the *linga* of Shiva) is a square cella; above it rises a pyramidal tower that symbolises Mount Meru, the home of the gods. This part of the temple is the holy of holies, where the brahmins perform their rituals. These elements define the temple as such. In front of the tower or *shikhara* is a hypostyle hall called the *mandapa*, which generally has open sides and ends; in the centre of the *mandapa* the dances take place.

It is normally preceded by a courtyard reached through a *gopuram,* or gateway, which may attain monumental dimensions. The *shikhara* end of the temple is normally surrounded by a colonnaded gallery, which thus creates a corridor for ritual circumambulation. Though these are the main characteristics of the Hindu temple, infinite variation is possible. But it cannot be too strongly emphasised that the building has a symbolic meaning, which governs its forms and organisations: it is, before all else, the residence of the god.

All the component parts of the temple conform to a series of rules. At one level, this is a matter of plan and style; at another, the ornamentation of the temple derives from a long-established tradition. Some of these principles are simple: for example, the cella is square and stands in a square temple beneath a square tower, and the *mandapa* is strictly axial relative to the sanctuary. These two components create a symmetrical plan and are set within a courtyard on the same axis.

The Rules Governing the Plan and its Design

To these basic principles various imperatives are added. As the Hindu temple is the house of the god – this fact cannot be too often repeated – the priest-architects (*shthapati*) concern themselves with its positioning, orientation and the temporal circumstances of its construction. Even before the temple is built, a foundation ritual is required involving a study of the site and of the configuration of the heavens; on this will depend the choice of place and the date at which the first stone is laid.

The gravity of this enterprise is such that it requires procedures of ritual kind. The stars must be consulted by an astrologer. The site must inspected by a priest-architect able to discern the benevolent or malevolent influences of the terrain; this would include the nature of the subsoil, the dampness or dryness of the site, its exposure to dominant winds, the drainage of the soil, and so on. The orientation will be chosen according to the type of temple to be built, the god to be accommodated and the environment in general.

The last point relates particularly to influences to which the temple will be susceptible in town or countryside. In a town, the architect must take into account the principles of Hindu town planning, which require a rigorously geometric layout. The site is also affected by the caste system, since castes each have their own quarters in the town. Thus the imperatives by which the temple is governed begin to take in Indian society as a whole.

The temple is built in the image of the created world and is therefore laid out in accord with the *mandalas*, elaborate magical graphic systems based on circles and squares. *Mandalas* form symbolic diagrams representing the universe in its cosmic evolution.

Thus a whole series of more or less coherent and logical imperatives governs the foundation of the temple. The same is true of the plan chosen by the *shthapati*. The plan of the sanctuary and, in particular, that of the cella, known in Sanskrit as the *garbha griha*, which must be square, is also determined by the *mandala*.

Behind this requirement lies the fact that all types of construction have a precise meaning in a symbolic world. The simplest forms carry a definite significance. Hindu cosmology is distinctive in that the circle represents the earth and irrational nature, and the square the sky and the cosmic order. For this reason, the square is the governing form for the habitation of the gods in its concrete form, the temple. And the *garbha griha*, which must represent the celestial world, are all of rigorously square plan.

The plan of the sanctuary is based on the square, but subdivided into a series of small square areas, each derived from whole numbers. Thus the side of the quadrilateral will be divided into 3, 4, 5, 6, 7, 8 or 9 parts. Its surface area will thus be 9 (3^2), 16 (4^2), 25 (5^2), 36 (6^2), 49 (7^2), 64 (8^2) or 81 (9^2) small identical squares. In this way the Brahmanic mathematician decides which scale the building is to be governed by. The scale literally informs the building structure. The name of each of the variants of the *mandala* is found in the southindian text *Mayamata*. The 8 by 8 unit (64 squares), for example, is the *manduka mandala*, while the 9 by 9 unit (81 square) is the *paramasayika mandala*. The *garbha griha* is generally governed by one of these two units.

In Hindu theological speculation, a correspondence was often sought between the squares of the *mandala* and the gods of the Hindu pantheon. Each square, therefore, has a sacred value. The northindian text *Brihatsamhita* goes further and envisages a demon within the 9 by 9 unit square: the Vastu Purusha drawing down at the command of deities and fixing the layout. This image is named the Vastu Purusha Mandala and is considered to have considerable cosmological value. The Vastu Purusha is a demon that got between heaven and earth and disturbed the cosmic order until the gods took control of the various parts of his body, thus changing his demonic character and preserving the order.

It would be of little interest to detail the properties of each *mandala* thus discerned as if through a transparent medium in the layout of any building. But it is important to realise that the procedure determining the building of a sanctuary is prescribed by an extremely complex magico-religious system.

This is codified in great detail in certain Sanskrit texts, such as the *Vastu-Sastra*, a theoretical treatise, and the *Mayamata*, a more practical compendium. Over the last few decades, authors such as Stella Kramrisch, D. N. Shukla and Bruno Dagens have described the basic principles involved, and summaries can be found in the works of Andreas Volwahsen and Louis Frédéric.

It should not, however, be thought that the system governing these architectural rules is a uniform and rational one. Certain of the prescriptions are of very ancient derivation and their sense seems not always to be clear. This is especially true of the astounding use made of the figures obtained after a series of divisions comprising a 'remainder'.

The irrationality of the remainder so fascinated the Indians that in due course they worked out a mysterious 'doctrine of the remainder' (as Volwahsen calls it). We might cite the analogy of the Greek fascination with squaring the circle. The pseudo-mathematical procedure requires that only the remainder of the division of

Above left

Mandala

Above: The *manduka mandala* (8 by 8 pada), which governs the plan of the *garbha griha* or *sanctum* of the temple.

Below: The *paramasayika mandala* of north India (9 by 9 pada) with the symbolic arrangement of the Brahmanic divinities.

Below left

Yantra

Above: A *yantra* representing the celestial city and its gates, with the symbol of Illusion set in a triangle within the lotus.

Below: The *yantra* of liberation. Within the square of the city, an octagon, a circle, a hexagon and triangles are inscribed one within the other.

Right

Mantra

1. Plan of a three-*ratha* (*triratha*) *shikhara* with three projecting elements on each side.
2. Plan of a five-*ratha* (*pancharatha*) *shikhara* with five projecting elements.
3. Plan of a *pancharatha shikhara* with external recesses and internal indentations in the *garbha griha*.
4. Plan of a tower with seven *rathas*, external recesses and triple internal indentations on each side of the *garbha griha*.

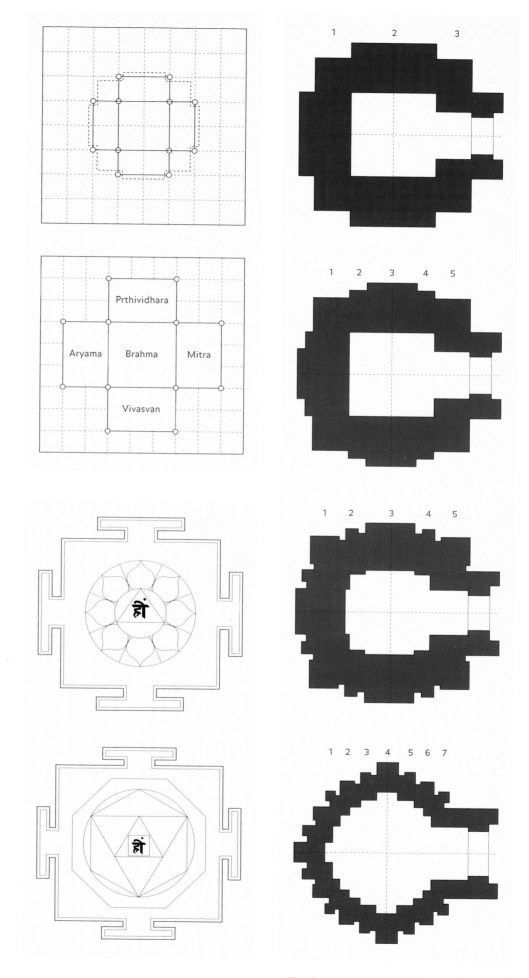

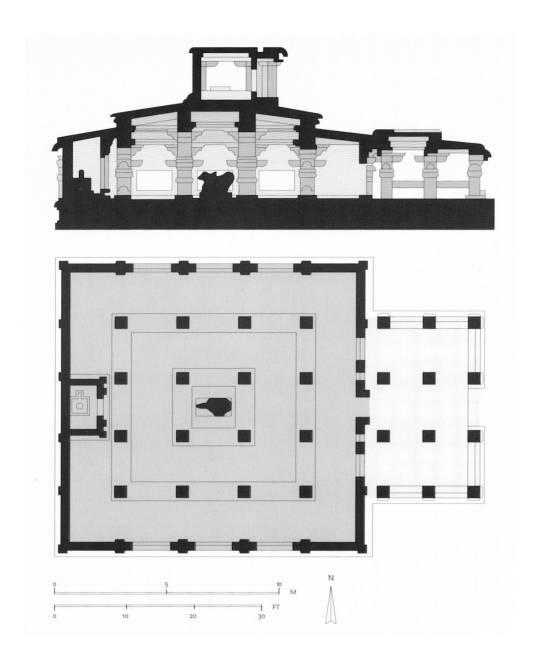

two numbers (forming a proportion, for example) should be taken into account when determining the length, breadth and orientation of a building. The remainder is therefore considered in its relation to the twenty-seven planets or twelve signs of the zodiac. Further elements in the calculation include the caste of the founder and the 'life expectancy' of the temple. This is not a perfectly coherent system.

Yet Hindu architecture is outstanding for its organisation, its extreme accuracy and rigorous planning and for its geometrical perfection. So obvious is this that one wonders if the magico-astrological mysteries are not simply intended to reinforce the authority of the esoteric millennarian tradition of architecture from which they proceed. The *shthapati* may perhaps have developed this recondite procedure in order to veil the absurdity of prescriptions whose origin and meaning had long since been forgotten.

To return to the plan of the temple: the *mandala* that governs the very sober outline of the cella with its subdivision into identical squares also specifies the thickness of the walls and their projections and re-entrants. This latter point is the origin of the many cusped vertical projections in a temple façade; they are called *rathas*.

The *mandala* applies not only to the cella but also to the temple as a whole – if not indeed to the city as a whole. The sanctuary is surrounded and protected by its

The entrance of the Ladh Khan Temple

An axial stairway gives access to the twelve-pillared vestibule of the oldest temple in Aihole, the capital of the Chalukya dynasty. The roof rests on sturdy, low pillars with intersecting corbels. On the roof, the little shrine prefigures the *shikhara* found in later Chalukya temples.

precinct, which may be double or even triple walled. The roof-tower rising over the cella represents the divine city and, in some degree, the axis of the world. In this way the courtyard and the peripheral colonnade, along with the external precincts, are seen as equivalent to the mountain ranges by which the universe is bordered. A processional avenue forms the periphery of the city, just as the peripheral corridor of the temple is the 'avenue' of circumambulation. There is therefore a quadruple analogy: the sanctum as such (the *garbha griha*), the temple as a whole, the city as a whole, and the universe. Stressing the continuity between nature and the residence of the gods on Mount Meru by linking the world to the deities, the magical outlines contrive to unite humankind to the gods and creation to the divine world. It is one of the characteristics of Hindu cosmological doctrine thus to create analogies between the different levels of reality.

Art historians discern two different styles of Hindu architecture, the southern, or Dravidian, style and the northern style, known as Aryan or Nagara. And there are of course intermediate styles inspired by both north and south.

Above left

An ornamental *jali* from the Ladh Khan Temple
The bays of the Ladh Khan Temple at Aihole are closed by stone screens whose openings form elementary geometrical lattice-work. This form of window was to have a lasting influence on Hindu temple architecture.

Above right

Traditional ornament in the Ladh Khan Temple
A detail of the ornament of the entrance pillars of the Ladh Khan Temple in Aihole. The rosette and drapery motifs are reminiscent of Buddhist reliefs.

The Birth of Chalukya Architecture

The Chalukya dynasty began in the mid-fifth century A.D. and certain of its descendants were still in power in 1200. The capitals at Aihole, Badami and Pattadakal saw the construction of a fabulous series of monuments.

The Chalukya territory lay between Kanchipuram and Ellora and constituted a centre of influence in medieval Indian art. Many artistic innovations originated here and spread their influence far and wide, while the contributions of the Pallavas in the south and of Orissa in the north-east were absorbed into Chalukya art along with northern influences.

Aihole is particularly significant in view of its two main temples, the Ladh Khan Temple and the Durga Temple. They illustrate two distinct variants in the development of dressed-stone Hindu architecture. The first, constructed between 600 and 650, owes its name to a Muslim hermit who took up residence there in the nineteenth century. The temple is square in plan but highly original; it comprises a double peripheral corridor surrounding the later addition of a sculpture of Nandi, the bull-emblem of Shiva. Its cella, also later installed, stands next to the back wall

Below

The search for new solutions in the Ladh Khan Temple
Side view of the Ladh Khan Temple at Aihole: its stocky outline emphasises its experimental nature. The architects of Hindu dressed-stone buildings were still finding their way. The wide windows of the temple are filled with lattice-like solid stone *jalis*.

of the temple. Sixteen columns support this quadrilateral structure, which is lit by holes pierced in the stone slabs. It is preceded by a vestibule with four central and eight outer columns, all of which rise from a low perimeter wall. This forms a sort of verandah and could have served as a *mandapa*. Access is via a staircase flanked by an elegant banister.

The Ladh Khan Temple is roofed with huge slabs laid almost flat, just sufficiently inclined to permit run-off. Stone battens between the roofing-stones helped to render the surface of the roof watertight.

This roofing technique would seem to be a primitive effort to replace the conventional thatched roof on a wooden frame with a stone roof. Roofing-stones are common enough in Aihole; but they subsequently disappear from Hindu architecture to be replaced by successive layers of horizontal corbelling. The squat square-section pillars carry the considerable weight of the roof via a system of capitals composed of four sturdy brackets arranged in a cross-shape. These, too, would seem to be wooden brackets in petrified form.

The decoration of the Ladh Khan Temple includes handsome *jali* – stone slabs whose perforations compose geometrical motifs – and relief sculptures, now heavily eroded, on the columns of the vestibule. *Kudu* friezes run around the upper part of the temple base and around the sides of the roof to confer on the building the prestige of the celestial city. On the summit of the roof, a little square aedicule has reliefs of the three divinities: Vishnu, Surya and Devi.

The interior of the Ladh Khan Temple
Dominated by Nandi the bull added later (just visible in the central square), the Ladh Khan Temple at Aihole has a very ample circumambulatory space.

The Durga Temple in Aihole
Dating from between 675 and 725, the Durga Temple at Aihole is dedicated to Vishnu. It is clearly influenced by Buddhist *chaitya* halls. An external portico of pillars surrounds its apsidal *garbha griha* (above and below right), around which an open-sided circumambulatory gallery runs. The temple's sculpted decoration includes figures of great elegance (below left).

Buddhist influence in the Durga Temple

With its apsidal plan and external portico, the Durga Temple at Aihole resembles Buddhist *chaityas*, in which the 'apse' accommodated a *stupa*. A vestibule leads into the eight-pillared hypostyle hall that precedes a horseshoe-shaped cella intended to contain the statue of the god. Above it is an embryonic *shikhara*.

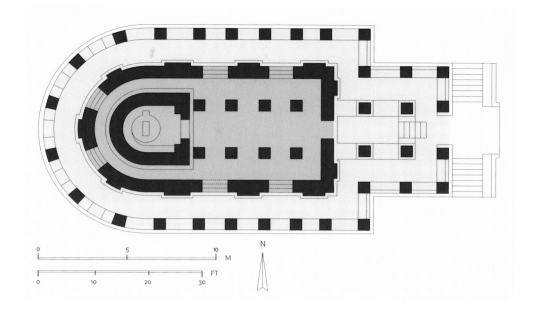

The Durga Temple dates from about 675–725 and is rather unusual in plan. Its peripheral colonnade itself has an apse, which encloses a structure of the same shape containing a hall, in which two rows of four columns form a nave and side aisles. The apsidal formula is reflected in the cella, which stands in the centre of the apse, leaving a narrow corridor for circumambulation. The layout adopts some elements of the plan of a Buddhist *chaitya*.

In front of the sanctuary, an entrance portico slightly narrower than the temple is reached by two staircases at right angles to the temple axis. In the portico, a series of columns rises from the low perimeter walls. Graceful deities, treated in a vigorous style of relief carving, ornament the pillars, which are capped with bracket capitals.

The overall appearance of the Durga Temple of Aihole is somewhat unusual. Its colonnade and apse relate it to Buddhist sanctuaries, while its high base and open bays confer on it an airy quality. Moreover, the partly ruined tower is remarkably unassertive and even a little incongruous. These exceptional qualities make the Durga Temple – together with some other very badly ruined monuments – somewhat in a category of its own. It was an architectural experiment with few successors.

A third Chalukya temple at Aihole also deserves mention. It is the main temple in the isolated Hucchappayya Matha Group, and probably dates from the end of the seventh century. It is roofed with large slabs and its walls are almost entirely blank, though its corner pilasters and door-posts are ornamented with elegant sculptures. *Kudu* motifs alluding to the city of the gods are prominent in the outline of the temple.

Primitive temples at Aihole
Aihole has many temples. Those of the Hucchappayya Matha group are low and stocky. They are roofed with stone slabs and date from the late seventh century. The sculptures that decorate them are reminiscent of the Gupta style.

From the Classical *Contrapposto* to the Ionic Temple of Taxila

The bronze figures of South Indian Chola art are notable for the animated motion of their hips. For a long time, their elegant pose was attributed to a direct influence from Hellenistic sculpture. And although today the hypothesis of direct influence tends to be rejected, it cannot be denied that there were certain political and economic connections between the Mediterranean and India which encouraged cultural interchange.

Greek sculpture went through a fundamental transformation at the beginning of the fifth century B.C. The frontality and stiffness that had predominated in Sumerian, Egyptian and early Greek art was eliminated at around this time thanks to a simple device termed *contrapposto*. The weight of the body was shifted on to one standing leg, while the other one, the trailing leg, either stepped forward or trailed behind with a slightly bent knee. Inevitably, realistic natural movement required that the hip and, later on as well, the shoulders be correspondingly tilted. The sculpted figure now seemed to be swaying to the rhythm of its own movement.

This pattern of movement must have originated before 480 B.C., since already in the so-called Persian debris in the Acropolis at Athens (the mound of demolished works of art left behind by the Persians after their capture of the Acropolis in 480 B.C. which later served to provide materials for new foundations during reconstruction), a statue was found featuring a slight tilting of the hips with one leg placed in front: the so-called 'Kritios Boy'. This pattern of movement later became the basic posture to be found in numerous statues of later antiquity, as can be seen in the illustration showing 'Agias' (a later copy of a work by the fourth-century sculptor Lysippos).

The adoption of *contrapposto* in Indian art probably occurred as early as the Hellenistic period. Alexander the Great's conquests had led him all the way to India; however, the resulting Hellenistic kingdoms that were established in the Near and Middle East were to be of even greater importance for cultural exchange – especially the Greek-Bactrian kingdom lying at the Western borders of the Indian world.

Conveyed through intermediate Indian-Greek cities in Bactria and Arachosia such as Taxila, Bactra and Begram, *contrapposto* also came to predominate in early Buddhist figures. Those in the *torana* of Sanchi from the first century B.C. show a distinct tilting of the hips. Adopted by Hindu art, this posture spread to the whole region of the southern Deccan, where it was particularly evident in Chola bronzes.

Foreign architectural forms arrived in southern India along the same route as *contrapposto*. For instance, among the ruins of Jandial near Taxila there are remains of a temple from the second century B.C. which can apparently be reconstructed as a Greek-style temple complete with Ionic columns and scroll capitals. The individual stages along this eastward-leading road of influence can be exactly traced by studying buildings in Hatra (Iraq), Kangavar (Iran) and Ai-Khanum (Afghanistan).

There is another architectural characteristic that is widespread in the Mediterranean and at the same time typical of southern Indian temples: the roof of the central square *mandapa* is often made up of stone slabs in superimposed layers, jutting out and each turning on a 45° angle. This roof construction (which Auguste Choisy termed the 'corbelling Lydian roof with slanting edge' in his treatment of the sepulchral chamber of the Hellenistic tomb at Belevi, Turkey) was also used on Roman graves, for instance in the mausoleum of Mylasa (Turkey). The false lantern dome, which can often be found in Indian architecture, is presumably a transference into stone of the ceiling beams from wooden constructions. In a Buddhist context, however, it can probably be attributed to Western influences.

From Greece to India
Left: Contrapposto first appears in Greek art in the fifth century B.C.: a marble sculpture of the late fourth century. (Delphi, Archaeological Museum)

Centre: A ninth-century figure from Khajuraho.
Right: The 'lantern dome' derives from models in Caria (Western Asia): the mausoleum of Mylasa, second century A.D.

The Temples of Pattadakal

In the former Chalukyan capital of Pattadakal (the City of the Coronation Rubies) there is an impressive group of temples dating from the eighth century. The Pallavas and Chalukyas were rival dynasties that battled for control of southern India. But in the wake of war artistic influences were exchanged and the result was a style that combined Dravidian and Nagara styles.

The ruined Galaganatha Temple, one of the earliest temples, contains elements of north Indian monuments. But the Pallava influence in the little Sangameshvara Temple (circa 725) is visible at first glance. Indeed, the Sangameshvara Temple has clear references to the Arjuna Ratha at Mamallapuram, the difference being that the Pattadakal temple is of dressed-stone rather than rock-cut, like the Kailasanatha Temple at Kanchipuram. And the stepped layers of the pyramidal roof exhibit the same miniature edifices.

About 745, two remarkable temples were built simultaneously by two sisters in commemoration of the victory of their husband Vikramaditya II over the Pallavas. They are known as the Mallikarjuna and the Virupaksha Temples. It seems likely that the same architect was responsible for both; both are clearly in Dravidian style. The Virupaksha Temple has survived almost intact and is of particular interest. Its cella is surrounded by a narrow passage and gives on to a fine hypostyle hall with four bays of four pillars; a further two pillars precede the cella, forming a kind of porch.

The hypostyle hall forms the centre of the composition and is surrounded by three projecting portals, creating a most original cruciform plan. In front of the axial portal is a *mandapa*, built in 744, which accommodates the bull Nandi. It stands in the centre of a courtyard, which is entered via a gateway in the form of a low *gopuram*. The building is enclosed by a low wall that follows its cruciform plan.

Panoramic view of the site of Pattadakal
One of the capitals of the Chalukya dynasty, Pattadakal is the site of a series of remarkable temples. Separated by the *shikhara* of the Kasinatha Temple, which dates from the late seventh century, stand the Sangameshvara Temple (circa 725), dedicated to Shiva, and the Mallikarjuna Temple (mid-eighth century, right). Behind the Mallikarjuna Temple can be seen the tower of its contemporary, the Virupaksha Temple; both stand in their own courtyard.

Page 75 below
Dravidian style in the Sangameshvara Temple
The Sangameshvara and Virupaksha Temples at Pattadakal both have a square summit (*stupi*). This reflects the Dravidian style, whereas the tower of the little Kasinatha Temple, with its convex corner-profiles, shows the influence of the Nagara (northern) style.

Page 76

A debonair *dvarapala* of the Mallikarjuna Temple

The Mallikarjuna Temple at Pattadakal is a typical Chalukya temple. The view here is from the *gopuram* that leads to its 'twin', the Virupaksha Temple. Carved divinities cover its façade. Above them, miniature edifices embody the theme of the cosmic mountain.

Narrative reliefs in the Mallikarjuna Temple

The relief carvings on the pillars of the Mallikarjuna Temple (built around 745) at Pattadakal depict scenes from the *Mahabharata* and *Ramayana*. The vivid narrative style resembles that of a strip-cartoon.

The shadowy interior of the Mallikarjuna Temple

Supported by twenty elegantly carved pillars, the *mandapa* of the Mallikarjuna Temple at Pattadakal is a fine example of the hypostyle halls of medieval Indian architecture, with their heavy lintels, weighty capitals and impressive roof-structures.

The end of the Virupaksha Temple
Reached through its own *gopuram*, the Virupaksha Temple, which was built circa 745, displays projections and re-entrants whose vertical rhythms contrast with the vigorous horizontal mouldings of its base. A multitude of divinities inhabits its recesses and aedicules.

The sinuous figures of the Mallikarjuna Temple
The reliefs of the Mallikarjuna Temple at Pattadakal resemble Chalukya sculpture. The carving of this delightful *contrapposto* nymph deploys a characteristically fluid, sinuous outline.

The hypostyle hall of the very similar Mallikarjuna Temple also has four bays of square pillars. Its interior has splendid sculptural decoration, in which scenes from the *Ramayana* and *Mahabharata* are prominent.

The external statuary is also of great subtlety and elegance, especially in the figures of the gods with their characteristically swaying hips.

By now Indian sculptors had achieved almost complete mastery in the portrayal of the human form and were able to model it with perfect anatomical coherence under transparent clothing.

The *mandapa* of Shiva's vehicle in the Virupaksha Temple
At the centre of the courtyard of the Virupaksha Temple at Pattadakal stands a pavilion sheltering the statue of the bull Nandi, symbolising Shiva's presence. The pavilion dates from 730–740 and is of sober design.

The cruciform plan of the Virupaksha Temple
Standing within a huge walled courtyard, the Virupaksha Temple is rigorously symmetrical in plan. On the axis of the *gopuram* that leads into the courtyard stand the square Nandi pavilion, then the great hypostyle *mandapa* that precedes the sanctum. The *garbha griha* is surrounded by a narrow circumambulatory corridor, with a courtyard forming a further peripheral passage.

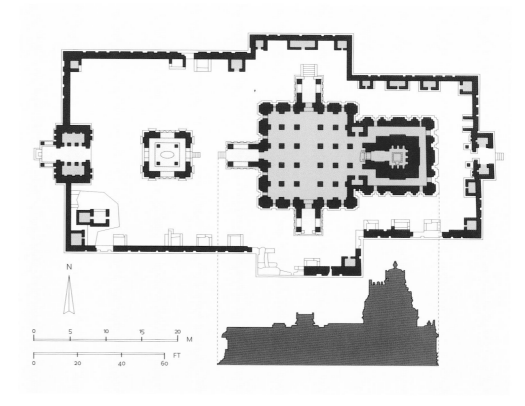

N

0   5   10   15   20
                          M
0   20   40   60
                        FT

Badami

Badami was formerly called Vatapi. It stands in an attractive setting formed by an artificial lake created by a medieval dam and is surrounded by a picturesque hillscape of red-ochre rock. The town offers a range of fine buildings, the earliest dating from the seventh and the latest from the ninth century. The site is also renowned for a series of caves entered through rock-cut galleries with sculpted pillars carved out of the cliff face; the earliest dating from the seventh century.

Just outside the present-day city of Badami lies the Malegitti Shivalaya Temple. It stands among a wilderness of tawny brown boulders and has survived more or less intact since the seventh century. The temple seems to have grown directly out of the natural rock in which its foundations are set and gives an impression of timeless stability. Its compact structure is clearly Dravidian in style, as witness the sturdy pillars of the porch and the massive capitals with crossed corbels (often in the form of modillions or volutes), whose very solid appearance is echoed inside the building. Other Dravidian features include the powerful layered corbels of the roof, the tower with its octagonal dome, the decoration of miniature edifices and the recurrence of the *kudu* motif on the profile of the temple.

Power rather than subtlety is the keynote here. It is countered by the graceful sculptures of Shiva (to whom the temple is dedicated), Vishnu, Krishna and the divine eagle Garuda. The windows are occupied by stone slabs with square perforations resembling lattice-work and surmounted by fine carved images of *makaras* or mythical aquatic monsters.

The ruined Azar Shivalaya Temple, built circa 600–650, dominates the mountain at Badami. Though its *mandapa* has been partly destroyed, its plan and decoration

The Malegitti Shivalaya Temple overlooks Badami
Overlooking another of the Chalukya capitals, Badami, the Malegitti Shivalaya Temple is of rather ponderous appearance. This is accounted for by its date: it was built circa 600, early in the development of the Dravidian style.

The weighty roof-structure of the Malegitti Shivalaya Temple
Detail of an 'inhabited' *kudu* from the Malegitti Shivalaya Temple at Badami that dates from circa 600. Influenced by the Pallava style, its roof-structure faithfully reproduces in stone the features of a timber-frame roof.

The decoration of the Malegitti Shivalaya Temple
The aedicule is at odds with the courses of dressed stone in which it is set, but the sculpture of Shiva between two dwarfs (*bhugatanas*) is already of a very high order.

The ruined Loval Shivalaya Temple
All that remains of the Chalukya temple of Loval Shivalaya at Badami (after 700) is its *shikhara*. The tower is dominated by an enormous octagonal *stupi*. The miniature buildings decorating the roof-storeys are notably abstract in style.

The Loval Shivalaya Temple dominates Badami
The tower of the Loval Shivalaya Temple rises from a rocky promontory that stands high above Badami. The space remaining to the left of the *shikhara* is very small and it seems likely that the *mandapa* was carried away in a landslide.

Relief in the Azar Shivalaya Temple at Badami
Detail of a relief decorating the base of the Chalukya temple of Azar Shivalaya (seventh century). The flower and tendril-like motifs perhaps derive from the Gupta style.

The Azar Shivalaya Temple on its eyrie
Seen from the Loval Shivalaya Temple, the Azar Shivalaya Temple displays an elegant profile on the heights above Badami.

Remains of the Azar Shivalaya Temple
Little elephants mark the entrance to the now roofless *mandapa* of the Azar Shivalaya Temple. Its vigorous *shikhara* forms a stylistic transition between the Malegitti Shivalaya and the Loval Shivalaya Temples. The abstraction of decorative forms is clear. On either side of the entrance to the *garbha griha* is a door leading into the circumambulatory passage.

Vaishnavite oratory
On the very edge of the artificial lake at Badami, under an overhanging rock, a little temple was built at 578. The building, part dressed-stone, part rock-cut, contains a relief of Seshasayi Vishnu: the god is asleep on the great serpent Sesha, who symbolises the cosmic ocean.

resemble those of the Malegitti Shivalaya, its near contemporary. The Loval Shivalaya Temple is of similar date, but only the cella and its roof (an octagonal dome-like structure with urn finial) survive intact.

The artificial lake forms an exquisite setting for the informal group of temples that stands on its shores. A guardian temple is set on the dam itself, like the chapels built on medieval bridges in the West. It is dedicated to Dattatreya, a divinity who combines the attributes of Brahma, Vishnu and Shiva. Considered no earlier than the twelfth century, it provides a fine illustration of a façade combining projections and re-entrants (*ratha*) with a strongly indented roof-line featuring the *kudu* motif. Its *mandapa* is bordered with square pillars, while the internal supports are stone columns worked on the lathe, using a technique commonly encountered even before the year 1000.

This technique is also to be found on the west bank of the artificial lake, in the charming Bhutanatha Temple from the thirteenth century. Its portico and *mandapa* display elegant columns made by a screw-cutting lathe. Resembling a child's top or a pile of plates of varying sizes, the sequences of cylindrical protuberances and

Dattatreya Temple on the dam
The dam that maintains the artificial lake at Badami has its own temple, intended to call down the protection of the gods upon the work and ensure its permanence. This is the Temple of Dattatreya, built after the twelfth century, a syncretic deity combining Brahma, Vishnu and Shiva. The columns inside the *mandapa* are made of stone turned on the lathe, while the pillars at its periphery are square. The oblong tower was built after the twelfth century and exhibits the southern influences which Chalukya architecture was then undergoing.

The elegant Dattatreya Temple
The little Dattatreya Temple at Badami is light and elegant in style. The multiple roof-storeys contrast with the vertical projections and re-entrants (*rathas*) surrounding the cella. The slender, graceful pilasters enhance the vertical tendency.

The roof of a hypostyle hall in Badami
The plain surface of the temple wall and the multiple storeys of the corbelled roof-structure form a striking contrast. The architecture of Badami was influenced by the Nagara style of north India. One of the features it adopted was the *pida*, a horizontal division corresponding to the corbels of the pyramidal *mandapa* roof.

undercuttings are interrupted by cubic elements. A similar treatment of the shaft of the column can be found 300 km further south, in the temples of Belur, Halebid and Somnathpur in Karnataka.

North of the lake, opposite the dam, a group of very picturesque older (apparently eighth- and ninth-century) temples display a combination of Pallava and northern features. Their Pallava-style towers have rather rudimentary *ratha* decoration, while the corbelled roofs of their *mandapas* are in the northern style. They are vivid illustrations of the convergence of influences in Badami, which is the birthplace of a mixed style. One of the charms of Badami is the architectural variety of its monuments.

The lighter style of the Bhutanatha Temple

On the west shore of the lake stands a temple that testifies to the stylistic development of Chalukya architecture. Later than the temples overlooking the town, the Bhutanatha Temple dates from the thirteenth century and has an open vestibule with an axial staircase. The building is still somewhat squat, but of notably lighter style.

The influence of the Hoysala style at Badami

The *mandapa* of the Bhutanatha Temple shows some similarities with Hoysala architecture, which originated circa 1000 in the southern Deccan. The columns have been shaped on the lathe, and the intersecting corbels above the capitals rest on light *abacuses*.

Between lake and mountain
This group of temples at Badami is right on the shore of the artificial lake. Quay, shrines, temples, Nandi *mandapas* and oratories form a sacred complex. Deployed in this spectacular and unspoilt environment, the charm of Chalukya architecture is undeniable. The *shikhara* of the main temple, which resembles that of the seventh-century Azar Shivalaya Temple, testifies to the great age of this miraculously well-preserved ensemble.

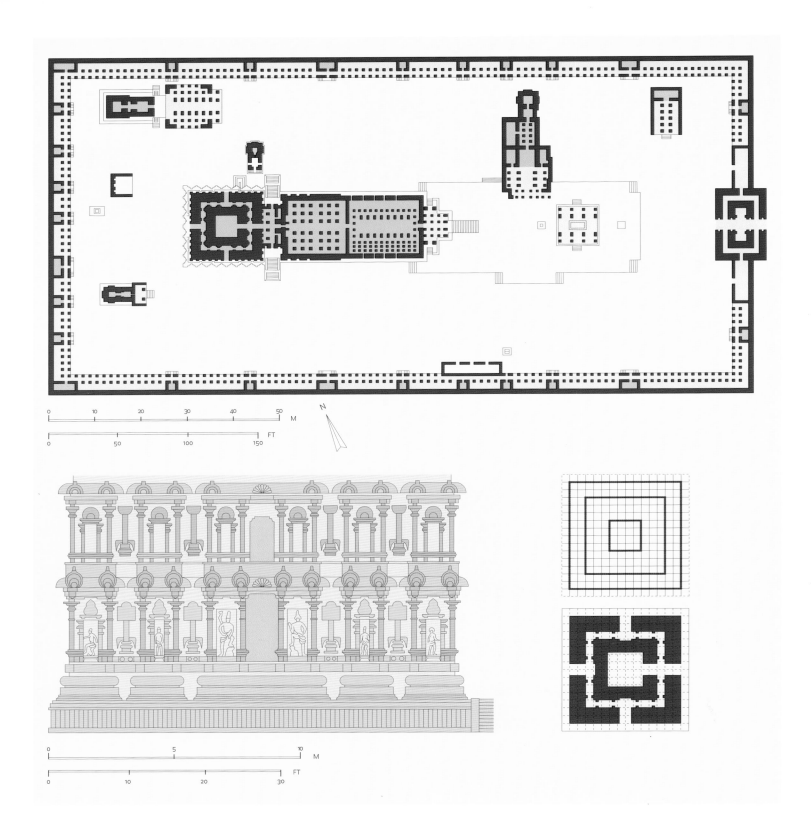

Above

Thanjavur: the majesty of the Chola dynasty

A general plan of the Shivaite Brihadishvara, or Rajarajeshvara, Temple at Thanjavur and its precinct. To the right is the *gopuram* giving entrance to the courtyard, which is bounded by a double portico. The temple, built at circa 1000, is preceded by a Nandi *mandapa*, then by two hypostyle pavilions. The tall *shikhara* covers a quare *garbha griha* round which runs a narrow corridor.

Below left

The rhythmic façade of the Brihadishvara, or Rajarajeshvara, Temple at Thanjavur

Elevation of the base of the *shikhara*. On both the lower level and second storey statues of the gods stand in aedicules.

Below right

The *mandala* of the Brihadishvara, or Rajarajeshvara, Temple

A *mandala* much favoured in southern India, the *padmagarbha*, governs the layout of the *garbha griha*. Left, the basic pattern and, right, the layout of the sanctum.

The *gopurams* of the
Brihadishvara, or
Rajarajeshvara, Temple
A perspective view of the portals
of the temple. To the right, the
great external *gopuram*; in the
centre, the second *gopuram*; and
to the left, the Nandi pavilion.
All were built in the early
eleventh century by the Chola
King Rajaraja I.

The Great Temple of Thanjavur

Much further south, in the Tamil Nadu, the ancient city of Thanjavur, formerly Tan-
jore, occupies an eminent place. It was formerly the capital of the Chola dynasty,
which held sway over the whole of southern India in the period 836–1267. Here
medieval Brahmanic architecture attained its culmination.

The great temple of Thanjavur was founded by Rajaraja I, a Chola king who
reigned from 985 to 1014. This was a time of Chola expansion on all fronts. Having
defeated their immediate neighbours, the Chola now advanced their sphere of
influence as far as Bengal, while there were Chola possessions in Sri Lanka and out-
posts in Java and Sumatra. Their trade network brought commerce with Burma and
south-east Asia and reached as far as Indonesia. The Chola dynasty was the major
economic and military power of the region.

The great temple at Thanjavur admirably reflects this prosperity, indeed opu-
lence. The foundations were laid about the year 1002–1003 and the presiding traditions were Chalukyan and Pallavan. But here the scale is considerably larger. The
planning of the temple was carried out with the greatest rigour and its design
reveals particularly intense symbolic connotations.

The temple is called the Brihadishvara (or Rajarajeshvara), and is dedicated to
Shiva. It is surrounded by two walled precincts. The first of them measures 270
by 140 m (37 800 m²) and consists of a high wall running along the banks of the
River Kaveri. The second consists of a portico with a double row of pillars enclosed
by a wall 150 by 75 m (11 250 m²).

This perimeter wall forms a sort of rectangular cloister, whose outline is determined by the two contiguous squares. At the centre of each of these squares is
the *mandapa* of the Nandi bull in the entrance courtyard and the cella of the temple
itself. Over the cella stands the enormous *gopuram* or tower, 60 m high and 15 m
square at its base. The *garbha griha* at its base measures no more than 5 m square. It

is surrounded by a thick wall within which a narrow corridor allows the priests to perform the ritual circumambulation.

This huge, almost solid block, capped by the innumerable stepped layers of the tower, conforms to a measurement of sixteen *pada*, comprising 256 units, which is native to southern India. It forms a grid interwoven with concentric circles in which is modelled the hierarchy of the divine world, with Brahma, the origin of the cosmos, at its centre, surrounded by the habitation of the gods, whose brick and mortar equivalent is the circumambulatory gallery. Outside this is the domain of humanity (corresponding to the precinct) and the outermost layer is that of the inferior beings (represented by the plinth on which the esplanade is set). The temple thus constitutes an analogue of the cosmic order.

The scale of Shiva's emblem, the linga, was increased in this temple to such a height that the priests could no longer perform the ritual in which the linga is annointed with milk and ghee and decorated with flowers; an upper gallery was required and the result was the creation of a second storey, with the two levels at the base of the tower receiving the same external treatment.

This consists of niches in which stand fine sculptures of divinities. The vigour of the statues of Shiva and his avatars offers formidable evidence of the expressiveness of Chola art. The mastery of the sculptor's art is similarly evidenced in the terrifying *dvarapalas*, the guardians of the gate, that stand on either side of the passage leading through the *gopuram*. The Brahmanic artists of southern India were absolute virtuosi in the art of working hard stone. On the entire periphery of the temple base are protomes of mythical animals – lions intended as guardian figures – that ensure the stability of the whole.

The pyramidal roof of the inner sanctum has innumerable miniature edifices, the traditional motif of temple models first seen at Mamallapuram. Here as elsewhere they symbolise the divine city.

The monumental gateway of the Brihadishvara, or Rajarajeshvara, Temple
The first *gopuram* of the Brihadishvara, or Rajarajeshvara, Temple. It is 30 m high and gives access to the first of two rectangular precincts, which measures 270 by 140 m.

Page 93
Decoration of the first *gopuram*
The sculpture that decorates the steps of the pyramidal roof is often enhanced with stucco, which must at one time have been painted in vivid colours. Here Krishna watches the *gopis* at their toilette in the river; they are as yet unaware that he has stolen their clothes.

Page 94
**The formidable granite tower
of the Brihadishvara, or
Rajarajeshvara, Temple**
Among the most impressive
achievements of the Chola kings
is the temple's pyramidal *shikhara*,
built in the eleventh century.
Above the two storeys of its
façade rise the multiple storeys of
its pyramidal roof, which is nearly
70 m high. At the summit is a
domed monolithic *stupi*; how it
was placed there no one knows.

**Access to the *garbha griha* of the
Brihadishvara, or Rajarajeshvara,
Temple**
At the base of the *shikhara* of the
Brihadishvara Temple, larger-
than-life statues of the divinities
set in aedicules flank a double
flight of stairs. This magisterial
entrance is typical of the impressive monumentality of a temple
in which the architecture of the
Cholas attained its highest point.

Before the entrance to the central sanctuary, a four-columned vestibule separates the sanctum proper from the great *mandapa* that precedes it. This handsome hypostyle hall is square in plan, with six bays of six columns each. It is itself preceded by a further, rectangular *mandapa*, which is somewhat later. Before this stands a twenty-columned porch accessible by three staircases. The whole is governed by a strictly axial and symmetrical organisation, which is disrupted only by some later additions.

The monumental scale of this complex should now be evident. Around it runs the double portico with its dozens of lingas arranged under corbelled vaults carried by a total of some 400 pillars. Behind this forest of lingas, the portico wall is covered in beautiful paintings, some of which may well be contemporary with the construction of the temple.

An Unprecedented Achievement

No Hindu complex had previously attained such huge dimensions nor required such a very large outlay. The tower is built entirely of granite, and capped with an enormous monolith weighing some eighty tonnes. Its emplacement is thought to have required the construction of an earthen ramp several kilometres long on which a 'wooden road' was built using scaffolding. The local forests provided the raw materials. The ramp would have required considerable stabilising, not only against sidewinds but also against the passage of the eighty-tonne weight dragged on rollers by elephants and men.

In the north of the courtyard, a temple dedicated to Subrahmanya was built in the seventeenth century. Despite its late date, it exhibits excellent workmanship, though the decorative elements are perhaps excessively ornate and the detailing sometimes borders on the finicky.

One cannot write of Chola art without referring also to the magnificent bronzes created by the sculptors who cast the cult statues. The greatest masterpieces date from the tenth and eleventh centuries and represent Shiva Nataraja dancing in his corona of fire, the lascivious Parvati and the delicate Devi. They are among the crowning glories of southern Indian art. In them the Hindu masters attained a peak of perfection in their treatment of the human body. These bronzes are the equal of the greatest masterpieces of classical antiquity.

Shivaite mythology in the Brihadishvara Temple
One of the paintings decorating the gallery that encloses the inner precinct of the Brihadishvara, or Rajarajeshvara, Temple in Thanjavur. It shows Shiva and his wife Parvati on the back of the bull Nandi, fanned by two formidable servants. The style of this medieval painting well illustrates the intense religiosity of the Tamil lands.

A secondary temple: the Subrahmanya Temple

Within the Brihadishvara, or Rajarajeshvara, Temple precinct stands another temple, the Subrahmanya. It dates from the seventeenth century and its rigorous composition is articulated around its slender engaged colonnettes. The roof-structure remains faithful to the step-pyramid formula rising to a domed octagonal *stupi*.

A draining tank outside the Subrahmanya Temple

The clarified butter used in the sacrifices offered to the linga drains out of the *garbha griha* by a stone duct into a square tank outside the temple. The orthogonal lines of the Subrahmanya Temple are not disrupted by the wealth of sculpted decoration covering its façades.

Shiva Dakshinamurti
Four-armed, Shiva adopts the position known as Dakshinamurti ('He who faces south'). His anterior hands form gestures of reassurance and request. This twelfth-century Chola bronze combines complexity and serenity. (National Museum of India, New Delhi)

Krishna, the mischievous adolescent
Smiling and sprightly, Vishnu's avatar steps forward to bring joy to the believer. He is the incarnation of love and the destroyer of evil. In this thirteenth-century Chola bronze, he is the very image of cosmic serenity and possessed of a sinuous strength that delights the eye. (National Museum of India, New Delhi)

The beauteous Sita
Rama's consort is seen here wearing sumptuous ritual jewellery and a high hair ribbon. Sita is the perfect wife and the heroine of the *Ramayana*. This tenth-century Chola bronze incarnates the femininity of Dravidian India. (National Museum of India, New Delhi)

THE TOWERS OF BHUBANESHWAR

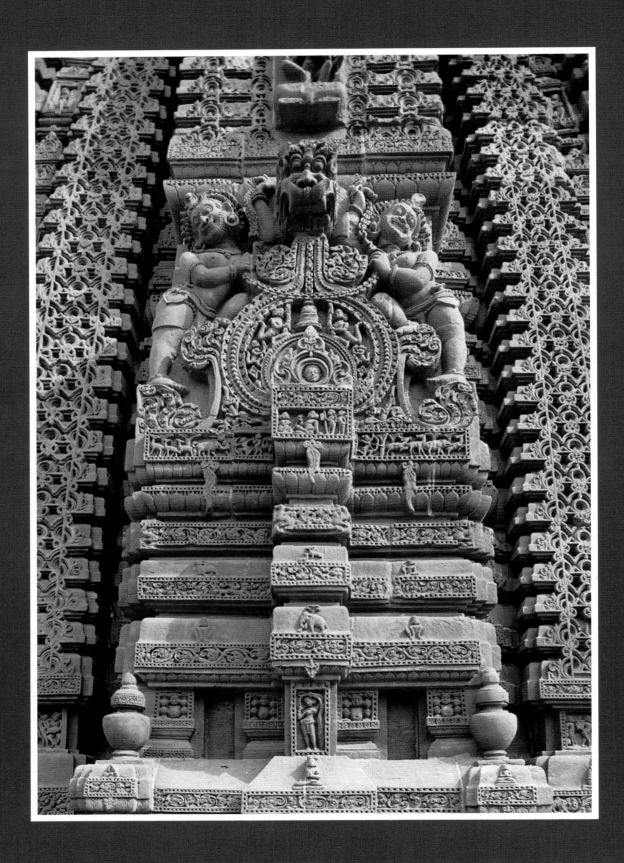

The Eastern Indian Aesthetic

Page 103

A magical treatise

Drawing from the cover of a treatise on *yantras*. *Yantras* are esoteric cosmological diagrams, based on the Hindu doctrine of Tantra. This eighteenth-century manuscript opens with a good-luck *svastika*, which symbolises the movement of the world and the stars. (Musée d'Ethnographie, Geneva)

The huge state of Orissa in north-east India lies on the shores of the Bay of Bengal. Formerly called Kalinga, its religious and artistic capital was the city of Bhubaneshwar. Tradition has it that, in medieval times, the temples of Bhubaneshwar numbered seven thousand. It is the heartland of one form of the northern style, or Nagara style, which spread through the north of the sub-continent, and fused on the southern edge of its range with the Dravidian style. From Gujarat to Rajasthan, not far from the Gulf of Oman, it reigned supreme.

The prosperity of Kalinga antedates Christianity. When the Emperor Ashoka attempted to invade the region in the third century B.C., he met ferocious opposition. It is said that the carnage of this war so disturbed Ashoka that he turned to Buddhism, of which he became the official patron, and that he thereafter sought to banish violence from his realm.

The Caves of Udayagiri

In the first century B.C., King Kharavela from Khandagiri and Udayagiri ruled Kalinga, near Bhubaneshwar. A member of the Cheta dynasty that ruled from the second to the first century B.C., he converted to Jainism, and his court and most of his subjects followed his example.

Jainism was founded in the sixth century by Mahavira, who received the appellation 'Victorious' (Jina) because his ascetic lifestyle had taught him to see into the essence of being. His reform of Vedism is contemporary with that of the Buddha. It found expression in an atheistic cult founded on respect for life, truth and chastity; the product of this respect is purity.

Jainism proved very popular in Kalinga. Kharavela celebrated his faith by decreeing the excavation of a series of caves out of the surrounding hills. Many of the temples have come down to us in an excellent state of preservation. Thus the Rani Gumpha Complex, which rises to two storeys, with ranges of cells on two adjoining sides of a vast central courtyard, was designed as a residence for monks. The doors of the cells on the lower storey have engaged columns that seem to support tympanums within stone arches. Abundant sculpted decoration, now badly eroded, enlivens this level.

On the second level, the cells give on to porticoed passageways and the sculptures were thus protected from erosion. Above the 'arches' are carved hunting scenes and processions of elephants. The elephant theme is also present in the Ganesha Gumpha Cave. But there, two sculptures in the round represent the elephant.

Thus in eastern India, on the same latitude as Elephanta and Ellora but at a somewhat earlier date (first century B.C.), rock-cut architecture gave powerful testimony of its architectural and artistic qualities. The temples constitute a sort of echo of the earliest creations, which were somewhat further north, in the Barabar Hills of Bihar. These date from the third century B.C., and there, too, the sculptors represented processions of elephants; they are to be seen at the entrance of the Cave-temple at Lomas Rishi, which was perhaps founded by Ashoka himself.

Decoration of a *shikhara* in Bhubaneshwar

The Mukteshvara Temple in Bhubaneshwar, dating from the second half of the tenth century, has a richly decorated tower with convex faces. The axial band of vertical panels (*rathas*) exhibits the classic *candrashala* motif in the form of a window; on either side of it stand guardian genies. The prolixity of the ornament is typical of medieval Orissan art in the Nagara style.

A Harvest of Temples

The Brahmanic renaissance of the sixth and seventh centuries led to a great upsurge of Shivaism too. In Bhubaneshwar, its popularity led to the creation of a new and original form of temple. Trade between Bhubaneshwar, Burma and Sri Lanka was flourishing at this time and supported this architectural achievement, which naturally absorbed considerable resources.

One of the characteristics of the Nagara style is the convex profile of the tower or *shikhara*, known in Orissa as the *rekha*. The rounded lines rise in an elegant hyperbola to a flat, cylindrical summit, on which stands an urn-shape, which is the jar for the nectar of immortality (*amrita*).

The façades of the tower are divided vertically by deep symmetrical re-entrants; these alternating projections and re-entrants are dictated by the *rathas* (cusped projections) of the square sanctum containing the cella. The channels or grooves running down the towers are sometimes so deep as to delineate subsidiary towers (*pagas*) abutting and buttressing the central tower. The result is a tightly bound sheaf of richly decorated elements that replicate on a smaller scale the central mass and emphasise the upward dynamic of the tower.

The verticality of the tower is contrasted with the horizontality of the *mandapa*, the dance-pavilion, known in Orissa as the *jagamohana*. The *jagamohana* is the opposite of the *rekha*. The *rekha* forms a sheaf of verticals whereas the *jagamohana* roof is created by 'stacked' corbelling and its horizontality is accentuated by deep grooves called *pidas*. This corbelling in dressed stone gives form to the pyramidal stone roof-structure of the *jagamohana*, which is usually wider than the base of the tower even at floor-level. The juxtaposition of these two architectural components, one horizontal, one vertical, defines the Orissan style. The link between the two elements is made by a simple corridor, as if the addition of a second element were an afterthought.

Of the many Nagara temples of Bhubaneshwar (of which a great number are partly ruined) we shall analyse some half-dozen. All were built in the period A.D. 700–1250 and all mark representative steps in the development of Hindu architecture in north-east India.

A hymn to life at Udayagiri
The low-reliefs decorating the
Udayagiri cave-temples, near
Bhubaneshwar, illustrate Jain
legends in a style much influenced
by Buddhist art. Animal life is a
further theme in the Rani Gumpha
Cave-temple. The reliefs form a
continuous motif running
between the arches over the
doors of the monks' cells.

**Façade and plan of the Rani
Gumpha Cave-temple**
The Jain Monastery of Rani
Gumpha at Udayagiri dates from
the second century B.C. and
resembles the Buddhist *viharas*
of Ajanta and Ellora. It is on two
storeys, all carved from the rock;
the arches apparently supported
by engaged pillars give the appearance of wooden architecture.
The plan of the two storeys shows
the portico now missing at first-
storey level.

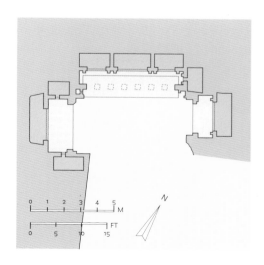

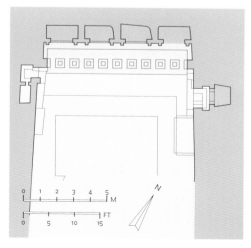

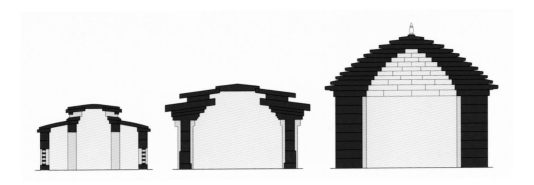

Sections showing the development of the *mandapa* in a series of
Hindu temples in Bhubaneshwar:
hypostyle pavilions of the eighth,
ninth and twelfth centuries. The
endpoint is the corbelled roof
comprising a succession of horizontal levels (*pidas*).

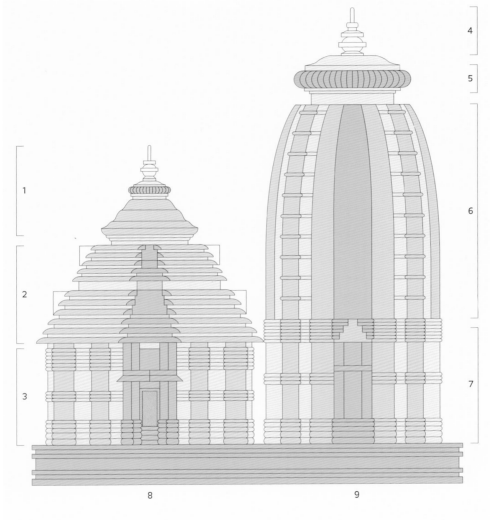

Terminology of Nagara temples in Orissa

1 The vase-shaped *kalasha* and the *ghanta* crowning the roof-structure of a *mandapa*, here called *pita deul* or *jagamohana*
2 The successive levels of the horizontal *pidas*
3 The outer wall, or *bada,* of the dance pavilion
4 The *kalasha* crowning the tower or *rekha deul*
5 The *amalaka*, a fluted disk bearing the *kalasha*
6 The central area of the tower with the vertical lines formed by the *pagas*
7 Wall of the sanctum, or *bada*
8 Elevation of the *pita deul* or *jagamohana*
9 Elevation of the *rekha deul*
10 Plan of the *jagamohana* or hypostyle pavilion
11 The sanctum, or *garbha griha*
12–16 The series of projections and re-entrants (*rathas*) of the tower, forming the *pagas*. The *konaka rathas* (12 and 16) are the corner *rathas*, the *anardha rathas* (13 and 15) intermediate, and the *raha ratha* (14) is central.

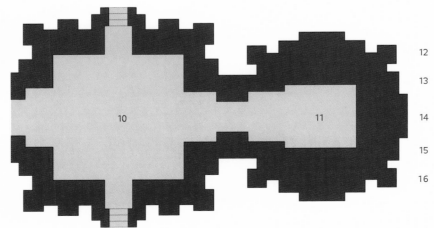

A primitive temple: the Parashurameshvara Temple at Bhubaneshwar

The *jagamohana* of the Parashurameshvara Temple (650–700) at Bhubaneshwar is very low and its roof-structure features only one horizontal recess (*pida*). The tower, by contrast, already displays all the features of the *rekha deul* of the northern Indian Nagara style in its Orissa variant, notably its convex faces. Its ornamentation is exquisite.

The *jagamohana* of the Parashurameshvara Temple

The assembly or dance pavilion of the Parashurameshvara Temple at Bhubaneshwar is extremely sober. Its square pillars are undecorated and its weighty capitals carry a slightly raised central 'nave'. At the back is the *garbha griha*.

From Experiment to Classicism

The little Parashurameshvara Temple, dated by some to 650, by others, more plausibly, to the late seventh century, stands beneath a large tree and has undergone a remarkable restoration. Its low *mandapa* has no base, and its tower is somewhat squat. But it already presents all the characteristics of the *rekha* with its convex lines.

It is a relatively small building, measuring 15 by 6 m, and the tower no more than 13 m high. The dance hall (*jagamohana*) betrays its early date by having only two levels of corbelling. So it lacks the deep horizontal grooves (*pidas*) that mark the pyramidal roof of the standard Nagara *mandira* – and the hall is not square but rectangular. The tower has three vertical parts of the wall or *pagas* on each face, and is therefore categorised as *triratha*. The central part of each side of the *shikhara* projects slightly, accentuating the upward movement of the building.

The luxuriant ornament clothes every stone of the tower (whose courses are visible from the outside) and is very striking. The *kudu* or miniature window motif is omnipresent, with small figures emerging from the windows, while nymphs and divinities crush monsters and vigorous lions mount guard on the sides and summit of the tower.

There is a side entrance in addition to an axial door, but most of the light in the *mandapa* comes from the *claustra* of perforated stone (*jali*). The asceticism of the *mandapa* is in striking contrast to the exuberance of the deeply carved external walls. It has two rows of simple square pillars with heavy capitals, dividing the space into nave and aisles. The central area has a raised ceiling and is covered with stone slabs that span the entire area with the aid of some lateral corbelling.

The stonework of the tower is made up of relatively small, flat blocks. This may have been influenced by local modes of construction in which brick is combined with bamboo-frame structures.

This early example already presents all the characteristics of the Bhubaneshwar *rekha deul* (tower), though in rather abbreviated and clumsy fashion. By contrast, the *pita deul* or hall is still at an early development stage; the oblong plan is unusual relative to later examples and the roof-structure has only two levels of corbelling.

Coeval with the Parashurameshvara Temple is that known as the Vaital Deul. Here it is the tower that is atypical, not having adopted the standard square plan of the *garbha griha*. It is oblong in plan with a transverse barrel-vault roof similar to

Reflected in its tank, the Mukteshvara Temple complex
The Mukteshvara Temple at Bhubaneshwar dates from the late tenth century and is one of the most representative examples of the Nagara style in Orissa. The convex faces of its *rekha deul*, vertically striated with *pagas*, contrast handsomely with the horizontal *pidas* of the hypostyle pavilion.

those of the *gopurams* of southern India, notably Thanjavur. The *jagamohana* hall, like that of the Parashurameshvara Temple, has a roof made up of only two layers of corbelled slabs.

Here again, there is a remarkable sculptural organisation in the ornamental carving of the handsome, orange-tinged sandstone of Bhubaneshwar. Sculpture adorns the pilasters that cover the apse of the temple. Graceful nymphs occupy small niches and the capitals are decorated with pairs of lions dominating elephants. The virtuosity of the sculptors is everywhere apparent.

In the handsome Mukteshvara Temple, built in the second half of the tenth century, we encounter a more mature plan. It is, like the Parashurameshvara Temple, oriented towards the west. At its apse is a tank in which the faithful perform their ablutions.

The axial organisation of the Mukteshvara complex has permitted the juxtaposition of three elements. The precinct itself includes the Siddheshvara Temple, a *torana*-style portal in the form of an arch resting on two columns, and a second precinct. This is delimited by a low, delicately ornamented wall and is entered through the small but magnificent portal. The door of the temple itself leads into the *jagamohana*, the cruciform dance or meeting hall, which is slightly longer than it is wide. Through it one passes to the *garbha griha*. The sanctum containing the linga is a dark, windowless, cubic room within the base of the tower.

The square tower has convex sides and several cusp-shaped projections (*rathas*); vertical corbellings (*pagas*) emphasise its soaring height. On each side of the tower, four vertical grooves curving in towards the top reinforce this impression. On the platform at the summit of the tower, the heavy fluted disk of the *amalaka* interrupts this vertical movement, which is restored by the pot-like finial, called the *kalasha*, that surmounts it.

The carved ceiling of the Mukteshvara Temple
The assembly or dance pavilion of the Mukteshvara Temple is rectangular in plan. The octagonal form of the ceiling is made by stone beams set diagonally across the corners and then profusely carved. The levels seen from the inside correspond to the *pidas* visible from the outside.

The Mukteshvara Temple: a paradigm of the Nagara style
The Mukteshvara Temple is one of the most famous examples of Orissan architecture. It is renowned for the coherence of its design and the perfect balance between the tower and the dance pavilion. To reach the low-walled precinct in which the temple stands, the visitor must pass through an original *torana*, built around 950–1000 in the manner of a triumphal arch. Set on two sturdy columns with carved capitals, the arch seems to present a version of the *kudu* motif. It relies on cantilevered horizontal elements rather than voussoirs.

The proliferating decoration on the external walls of the Mukteshvara Temple exceeds in exuberance that of all previous temples. Everywhere there are sculptures, fine carvings, false dormers in *kudu* form, delicious female divinities with lascivious *contrapposti*, and lattice-like perforated *claustra* bordered with foliated scrolls and repeated motifs.

As to the *torana*, or honorific gateway with its heavy semicircular arch, this is built of courses of stone but lacks voussoirs and indeed all the features of an arch; it is a false arch entirely based on the principles of corbelling and lintels. The use of a semicircular arch strangely perched on two sturdy columns carrying capitals of much greater width than themselves is not unusual in the Hindu architectonic vocabulary. It is strange that the arch is not connected with other architectonic elements, but is isolated. The *torana* is intended to emphasise the importance of the entrance.

The ornamental repertory exhibited on the *torana* is very rich. It includes the two half-length *makaras* (fabulous fluvial beasts), reclining nymphs, *kudus*, garlands and engraved motifs testifying to the emblematic importance of the work. Great significance is attached to passage in almost all religions.

The roof of the *mandapa* is also deserving of attention. Here the pyramidal roof comprises eleven separate corbellings, forming the typical Orissa *pidas*. These successive horizontal layers make a very sober and peaceful impression. Within, the *jagamohana* is of rectangular plan, in contrast with the conventional square plan of later buildings. The succession of lintels over the angles of the square central span forms diamond motifs in imitation of the timber-frame roofing technique from which it derives, and the entire composition is covered in elegant and varied sculptures.

The Brahmeshvara Complex at Bhubaneshwar lies on the edge of a long, wide tank bordered with steps. The temple dates from about 1075 and stands within an indented rectangular precinct 36 by 25 m. Four smaller secondary temples at each of its angles are arranged on a *quincunx* (*pancayatana*).

The sanctuary is at the west end and very precisely oriented; on certain days, the first rays of the sun traverse the *mandapa* and enter the *garbha griha*. In the centre of the sanctum stands the linga of Shiva and in the centre of the square *jagamohana* stands a statue of the Nandi bull, Shiva's mount. The roof of the *jagamohana* is pyramidal and composed of eleven successive levels of corbels (*pidas*). It culminates in an enormous vase called *kalasha*.

The vigorous projections and re-entrants in the *rekha* now include smaller flanking towers. They are analogous to the miniaturised edifices ornamenting Pallava-style roofs in that both represent the residence of the gods on Mount Meru, the cosmic Mountain.

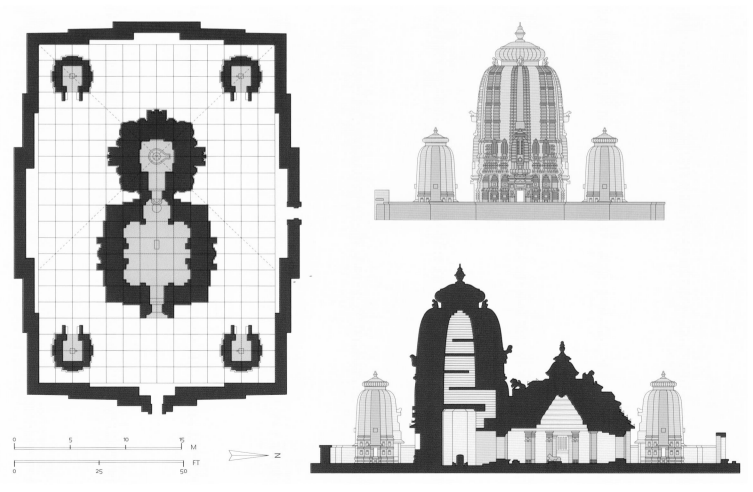

Visual structuring in the Brahmeshvara Temple
At the foot of the tower of the Brahmeshvara Temple (circa 1075), the play of horizontal and vertical emphases produces a clear structure. The base is carved as though with huge vases set side by side.

Page 117
A sheaf of parabolic lines: the Rajarani Temple
The tower of the Rajarani Temple exemplifies the irresistible vertical thrust of the Nagara style. The central tower is sheathed in smaller-scale replicas of itself.

Plan of the Rajarani Temple at Bhubaneshwar
The many projections (*rathas*) of the eleventh-century Rajarani Temple result in a diamond-shaped plan of the sanctum flanked by projecting turrets.

The Elegant Rajarani Temple

The next temple in our survey of the riches of Bhubaneshwar, the Rajarani Temple, was built in the eleventh century and marks a completely different kind of variant in Orissa architecture. Both the tower or *rekha deul* and the *jagamohana* or dance pavilion are radically transformed. The tower is now lozenge-shaped. Its mass is divided by the deep grooves that separate the flanking towers. The vigorous projections of the *pagas* emphasise the double axis of the tower. This complex sheaf of miniaturised towers tracing their convex shape against the convex sides of the central tower was to become the norm.

The temple structure now wears a completely new aspect. Its base is underlined by a row of motifs in the form of stylised vases. Above this are two panels decorated with alluring divinities, who exhibit a discreet eroticism as part of their natural elegance. The miniaturised external towers seem to clamber over each other to reach the summit of the central tower.

In the Rajarani Temple the influence of the central Indian style attains its full maturity – even if its culminating achievement is not at Bhubaneshwar, but at Khajuraho, further north, in the heart of India and in a region that was long cut off from the outside world.

The integrity of the new design is clear in the plan of the Rajarani's cella. A series of projections matching the disposition of the *pagas* on the outside of the temple makes the cella lozenge-shaped rather than cubic. The interior thus reflects the design that governs the exterior of the sanctuary.

The development of the dance pavilion or *jagamohana* is also complete. It measures 10 by 10 m and the internal space is bare of ornament. The square corbelled roof is made up of thirteen layers, exactly matching the thirteen horizontal grooves of the *pidas.*

The lozenge-shaped tower and square-plan dance pavilion are highly complementary. The two volumes, one soaring and vertical the other squat and solid, set each other off to most harmonious effect.

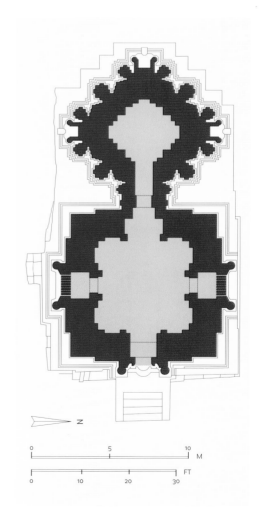

The austere interior of the Rajarani Temple
In contrast with the prolific decoration of the exterior, the interior of the Rajarani Temple's dance pavilion is almost ascetic. Above, the successive corbellings of the *pidas*; below, the junction of *jagamohana* and *garbha griha*. The architectural decoration is limited to the bare minimum.

The smile of celestial beauty
Under a palm branch symbolic of nature, the opulent and gracious forms of the *surasundari* evoke the splendours of the divine city.

The great Lingaraja Temple
The largest temple in Bhubaneshwar, the great Lingaraja Temple is closed to non-Hindus. It dates from the mid-eleventh century and its tower reaches 45 m. In this vast complex, sanctums and pavilions proliferate to form a holy precinct.

A Further Development: the Lingaraja Temple

The concept of the temple was gradually evolving in Orissa. In the Rajarani Temple, the link between tower and dance pavilion had acquired a clear dialectic and no longer seemed arbitrary, as it did in earlier examples of the formula. Temple architecture had found a form of articulation more coherent than mere juxtaposition. At the same time, a further development is discernible: that of addition, pure and simple. The huge Lingaraja complex (open, alas, only to Hindus) was erected in the mid-eleventh century and exemplifies the new principle. The procedure of addition by 'collage' is clear, as is the differentiation of functions. In this vast precinct, the central tower of the Lingaraja Temple emerges from a forest of smaller towers.

It is at once clear that this enormous place of worship must have been built in stages. The temple tower is 45 m high and its inner sanctum, which stands within a structure hollow from top to bottom, contains a baldachin carried on four pillars. The *shikhara* displays deep vertical re-entrants.

In front of the *garbha griha*, the rectangular *jagamohana* or meeting hall shares the cella's longitudinal axis. Four sturdy internal pillars support the *pida* roof. This is the classic arrangement, here completed by two further halls. The first, the *nata-mandira*, is reserved for dancing; open on to the exterior, it too possesses four internal pillars. The second hall, the *bogha-mandira*, or offering-hall, is on a larger scale, but follows the same pattern. Both are covered with pyramidal roofs.

The four buildings of the Lingaraja Temple are rigorously aligned. But the joints between them remain somewhat artificial; the *mandiras* give the impression of having been added one to another without constituting an organic unity. This is not a satisfactory aesthetic solution, but it was nonetheless influential; the Vaishnavite Ananta Vasudeva Temple, built in 1278, displays exactly the same arrangement.

A Reckless Enterprise: Konarak

At Konarak, 60 km from Bhubaneshwar, on the shores of the Bay of Bengal, rise the majestic ruins of one of the greatest of all Hindu temples, the Surya Temple or Sun God Temple, which was built circa 1240. Its *shikhara* was a colossal creation that was to have reached more than 70 m into the sky.

The enterprise was much too heavy for the friable soil on which it was built and the site was much too close to the ocean: the *shikhara* collapsed in the mid-nineteenth century. A similar fate awaited the dance pavilion, or *nata-mandira*, which here preceded the *jagamohana*; it has lost its superstructure entirely and now consists of a highly decorated base surmounted by pillars reaching up into nothing. In considering these two elements, we should note that, at Konarak, the architect abandoned the juxtaposition by 'collage' of the various parts of the temple and with it the arrangement adopted in the Lingaraja Temple at Bhubaneshwar.

Today the vast complex lies within a quadrilateral precinct and possesses axial *gopurams* and corner turrets. Of all this, only the *jagamohana* has survived almost intact. It is a square-plan building, 36 by 36 m and some 40 m high. The vast hall inside is no longer accessible, the entrances having been walled up and the whole reinforced, but, at something like 20 m square, it is one of the largest internal spaces in all Hindu architecture.

Its corbelled roof, carried on four mighty pillars, must have been some 30 m high. The imposing pyramidal roof has a row of three deep horizontal grooves (*pidas*) that

The principle of addition in the Lingaraja Temple
This simplified elevation and plan of a Lingaraja-style temple at Bhubaneshwar shows the juxtaposed halls preceding the *rekha deul* or tower. Left to right, the *jagamohana*, with its internal pillars, which serve as assembly room; the *nata-mandira*, a pavilion used exclusively for dance and music; and lastly, the *bogha-mandira* or hall of offerings. All three feature pyramidal roofs with horizontal steps (*pidas*).

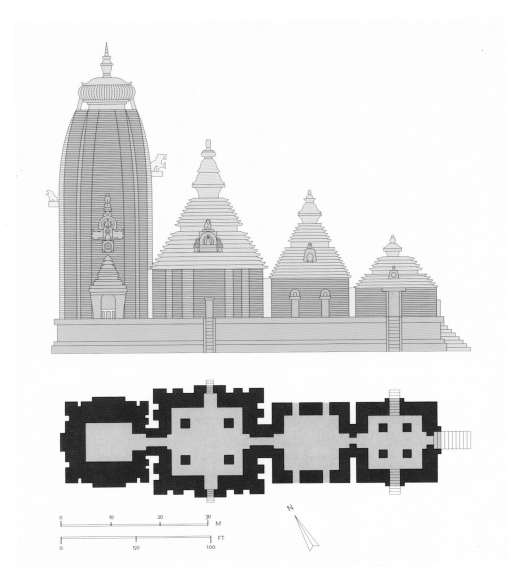

Two lions mount guard at Konarak
In the great temple of Konarak (circa 1240), two guardian lions overwhelm cowering elephants at the entrance to the dance pavilion (*nata-mandira*). The roof behind is that of the *jagamohana*; the *nata-mandira* has lost its roof.

Consorts of Surya at the Surya Temple of Konarak
The god of the sun, Surya, appears on the south face of the temple at Konarak (see page 124) flanked by his consorts and devotees in an admirable sculptural ensemble. Surya is a syncretic deity worshipped by Vaishnavite and Shivaite alike.

mark the step-by-step ascent towards the enormous vase or *kalasha* that decorates the summit.

The Surya Temple is set on a high base whose sides are covered in ornamental carving, including twelve pairs of enormous wheels, sculpted complete with hubs and spokes. Eight horses are sculpted in full relief on the sides of the entrance staircase.

The *jagamohana* thus comes to symbolise a colossal processional chariot. Huge wooden vehicles of this kind are commonly drawn in processions at great Hindu religious festivals; so the building is yet another example of the 'petrification' of a wooden design.

This 'vehicle' is the chariot of the sun, in which, according to Hindu mythology, Surya makes his daily circuit of the sky. In this, we see again how the Hindu temple is made to materialise an idea and establishes itself as a symbol of profound significance. When a processional chariot is taken out, musicians and dancers accompany it as it winds its way through the streets. Likewise, the musicians and dancers are portrayed amid the sculptures that adorn the temples. They are featured on the various levels of the pyramid (*pidas*) in the form of statues of beautiful, full-

breasted maidens and they are represented, too, by the innumerable nymphs to be found disporting themselves in the two registers of low relief carvings that decorate the *jagamohana* base. They form a kind of graceful garland thrown around the celestial vehicle, though the execution of the carvings is not always of the highest level.

One can only lament the loss of the tower of Konarak. For one can easily imagine the wonderful array of sculpture that would have ornamented this massive tribute to the sun god.

The formidable *jagamohana* at Konarak
Treated as an enormous processional chariot – in this case also the chariot of the sun – the great meeting hall at Konarak is the largest internal space created by Hindu architecture. Its pyramidal roof comprises three storeys of *pidas* and rises to 40 m. Behind it, a tower some 70 m in height collapsed in 1837.

The decorated base of the Surya Temple at Konarak
The huge terrace or podium of the temple at Konarak is decorated on all sides with projections and re-entrants, on which are carved little temples and celestial nymphs.

The immense *jagamohana* at Konarak
Plan (with *garbha griha* and tower restored) of the Surya Temple at Konarak. The corbelled hall was a technological *tour de force*, creating a space of 400 m².

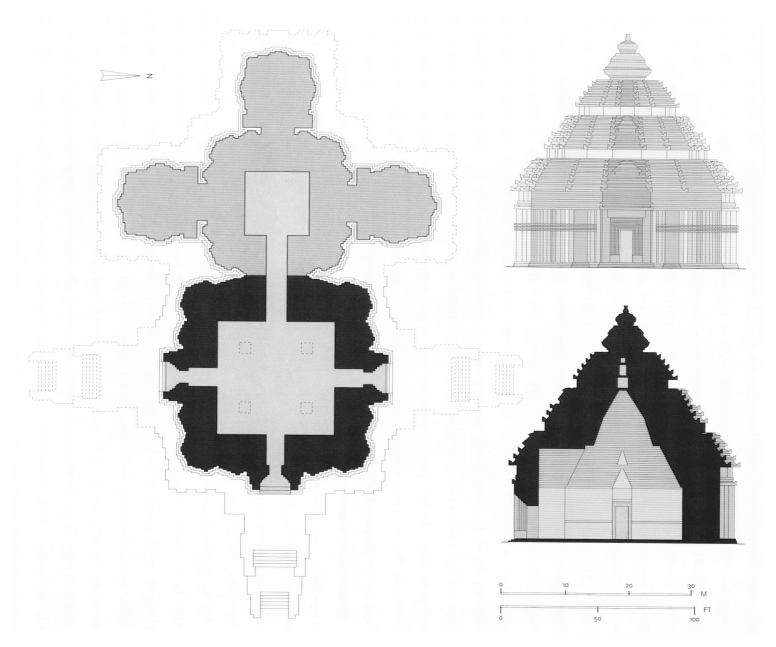

Surya looks south from his temple at Konarak
The colossal statue of Surya is sculpted in beautiful green meta-morphic stone. The god stands full frontal, static and hieratic, and the carving exhibits all the mastery of the sculptors of north-east India.

The vast wheels of the chariot of the sun
The entire base of the Temple of Surya at Konarak represents a petrified processional chariot drawn by seven sculpted horses. The smallest details of hub and spokes are reproduced in stone, and covered in luxuriant carved ornament.

The Architect and the Design

In primitive times, the temple was simply a sacred enclosure, defining the border between the domain of a god and that of nature. Later the divine habitation took the form of a hut containing the statue or effigy of the god. At this stage, its layout was subject to certain spatial imperatives contained in a symbolic diagram called the *mandala*. Its design became a *yantra* involving eight spatial directions in the form of eight deities. The temple was, at least in theory, oriented. In the east was Indra, the sky god; in the south-east was Agni, the god of fire; Yama, the god of death, was in the south; Nirriti, the god of poverty, in the south-west. To the west was Varuna, the god of water; Vayn was the god of winds and inhabited the north-west. Kunera, the god of wealth, was in the north, and finally Ishana, the Purifier, in the north-east.

A theoretical master or *shthapaka* was responsible for the overall layout and the religious concept of the temple. He prepared the site with certain rituals. The operation itself came under another building master, the *sthapati*. With the assistance of a master mason, a head sculptor and the master of the painter-decorators, he aided the *shthapaka*.

At the design stage, the project laid out by the *shthapaka* involved only measurements and proportions. Before proceeding to construction, the *shthapati* had to adopt a specific unit of measure. It might be a royal cubit, which was usual in temples, or an individual yardstick determined by the architect. This then became the common denominator of the proportions specified by the *shthapaka*.

The *mandala* governed horizontal proportions, but vertical dimensions also required determination. So for the tower, the base, the column and the crown were distinguished. The base formed a cubic volume. Then came the tall superstructure with its convex profile curving more steeply inwards at the top to form the summit platform. (This form, which is specific to the Nagara style, is said to derive from primitive creations in perishable materials, in particular from four large bamboo stems raised at each corner of the sanctum and tied together at the top.) This columnar part

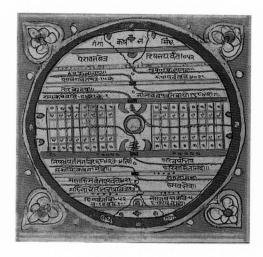

of the tower measured approximately two bases in height. The crown of the tower was composed of the great horizontal and round *amalaka*. At the centre of its indented periphery was raised a vase, the *kalasha*.

These, in a nutshell, are the rules governing the construction of a Nagara temple.

A representation of the world
Yantras are diagrams of the Indian cosmos. Geographical divisions and the mystical organisation of space find expression in motifs related to the plans of temples. Eighteenth-century manuscript. (Musée d'Ethnographie, Geneva)

THE CULMINATION OF MEDIEVAL ARCHITECTURE:

KHAJURAHO

A Consummate Architectural Achievement

Khajuraho undoubtedly owes its renown more to the sculpted decoration of its temples (which is often described as 'erotic') than to the intrinsic quality of its architecture. Yet these monuments, standing in a huge plain where the capital of a powerful kingdom once lay, are the greatest masterpieces of medieval Hindu architecture. The kingdom was that of the Chandellas, who ruled over the extreme north of the Deccan between the tenth and thirteenth centuries.

If the 'erotic' statuary of Khajuraho has eclipsed the merits of this incomparable architecture, the reason is to be found in the moral taboos prevailing in the West. The disconcerting aspect of the sculpture at Khajuraho is its 'scandalous' iconography. On the façades of several temples the carvings represent couples locked in sexual embrace alongside orgiastic groups.

The fact that these representations decorate a place of worship at first shocked Western visitors and subsequently occasioned a curiosity whose motives were not invariably or exclusively artistic. As a result, the buildings came to occupy second place in Western attention. A study devoted to the architecture of Hindu India must, clearly, attempt to reverse this emphasis.

As the crow flies, Khajuraho lies 800 km north-west of Bhubaneshwar and some 1000 km north-east of Elephanta. It is close to the valley of the Yamuna, the main tributary of the Ganges; the Jumna (Yamuna) flows through both Agra and Delhi. Under the reign of Dhanga (950–1002), the empire of Khajuraho extended as far as Gwalior in the west and Benares in the east. The city therefore enjoyed the influence not only of central and northern India but of the south too, and the result was the most perfect creations in the Nagara style.

The survival of the temples is due primarily to the decline of the country that began in the late eleventh century. They experienced numerous dangers: the raids of Muhammad of Ghor about 1200 were followed by the annexation of the province by the Sultans of Delhi in 1310. With its disappearance from the chessboard of Indian dynastic politics, Khajuraho saw its population diminish and the cultivated land around it became desolate. At the height of its prosperity, this dynastic capital was said to have possessed eighty-five temples; now it was of insufficient interest to attract conquest. At all events, the temples fell into oblivion and thus avoided the destruction caused by Islamic iconoclasm.

Unlike Mathura and Kanauj, prestigious capitals that were annihilated by Muslim armies, Khajuraho survived remote from the turbulence of history and was only rediscovered by the West about 1840.

The Earliest Temples

Today, there remain in the Khajuraho region twenty-two temples, some of them almost perfectly intact. We shall study only three or four of them, each one an essential step in the development of the Khajuraho style.

The earliest of them is the Chaunsath Yogini Temple, which must date from the origins of the city, before the tenth century. It is a very primitive complex of little granite shrines aligned around a huge courtyard measuring 31 x 18 m. This occupies an artificial esplanade and is accessible by staircases. It dominates a tank, which is now empty.

The square shrines, built in large rough-hewn blocks, have doorways made of monolithic jambs and lintels. The roofs are corbelled and constitute a sort of embryonic tower, with a convex curved outline anticipating the Nagara style.

Of the sixty-four cells that would seem to have been built for the sixty-four *yogini*, some of them animal-headed goddesses being connected with Tantric cults, only thirty-four still stand. They are of interest in introducing us to a primitive form of construction in large courses built without mortar. Their external walls – they all face the centre of the courtyard – display horizontal mouldings which underline their division into base, walls and roof.

These modest beginnings give little or no idea of the rapid development later shown by Chandella architecture. But the prototype of the mature temple architecture was built not long afterwards.

The Classical Model

At the entrance to the site of Khajuraho, the Lakshmana Temple offers a good illustration of the character of the sanctuaries built in the flourishing Chandella capital. (Lakshmana was the half-brother of Rama, who is an *avatar* of the god Vishnu and the hero of the *Ramayana*.) The Lakshmana Temple is also one of the most complete of the Khajuraho temples; its environment and overall design have survived intact. It was consecrated in 954, in the reign of King Dhanga (950–1002).

The temple is built entirely in sandstone and clearly shows the progress that had been made by that date. The building stands on a rectangular platform roughly 45 by 30 m. Four small temples stand at the corners of the esplanade, to which access is gained by an axial staircase on the eastern side. Two of these temples, framing the apse of the temple, open on to the east, as does the main temple; the other two face each other on either side of the entrance staircase.

The Lakshmana Temple is decorated around the entire periphery of its plinth with friezes of reliefs representing a procession in which horses, elephants, warriors, battle scenes and minor erotic themes can be seen.

The temple itself is on exactly the same plan as that of the most refined of these temples, the Kandariya Mahadeva, a plan echoed, with small variations, in the Devi

A primitive temple: the Chaunshath Yogini Temple
Built on a steep-sided esplanade, the ruined shrines of the Chaunshath Yogini Temple (holy place of the sixty-four *yoginis*) are primitive in style. They are among the earliest monuments of Khajuraho and probably date from the late ninth century.

The classical temple at Khajuraho
One of the temple complexes at Khajuraho. Left, the Matangeshvara Temple is partly screened by a smaller secondary temple that shares its podium. Right, the Lakshmana Temple, dedicated to Vishnu in 954. This sanctuary is one of the most accomplished expressions of the Nagara style, whose culminating achievements are found in central north India.

Jagadambi, the Parshvanatha, the Vishvanatha and the Chitragupta Temples. All of them have a vestibule (*ardha-mandapa*), dance or meeting hall (*mandapa*) and sanctum (*garbha griha*) forming a unified succession. All of them have towers with convex curvature, whose parabolic profiles reach up to the sky. And on each tower, the central body is buttressed by subsidiary turrets that rise in a sheaf towards the disk (*amalaka*) at the summit and the *kalasha* urn that crowns that. The high towers stand prominent on the flat horizons that ring Khajuraho, testifying eloquently to the multiplicity of temples erected by the medieval Chandella sovereigns.

Fully to comprehend the merits of this harvest of temples, we must analyse the most exquisite of them, the Kandariya Mahadeva. In it, the development of central Indian architecture reached a peak of perfection.

**The Lakshmana Temple
at Khajuraho**

On a platform decorated with a frieze of processing elephants stands the Lakshmana Temple, founded in 954 by King Dhanga. It is 33 m long and comprises a series of rooms with pyramidal roofs, culminating in the great *shikhara*. In the four corners of the podium are four small temples, together forming a group of five, like those of the Brahmeshvara Temple at Bhubaneshwar (circa 1075).

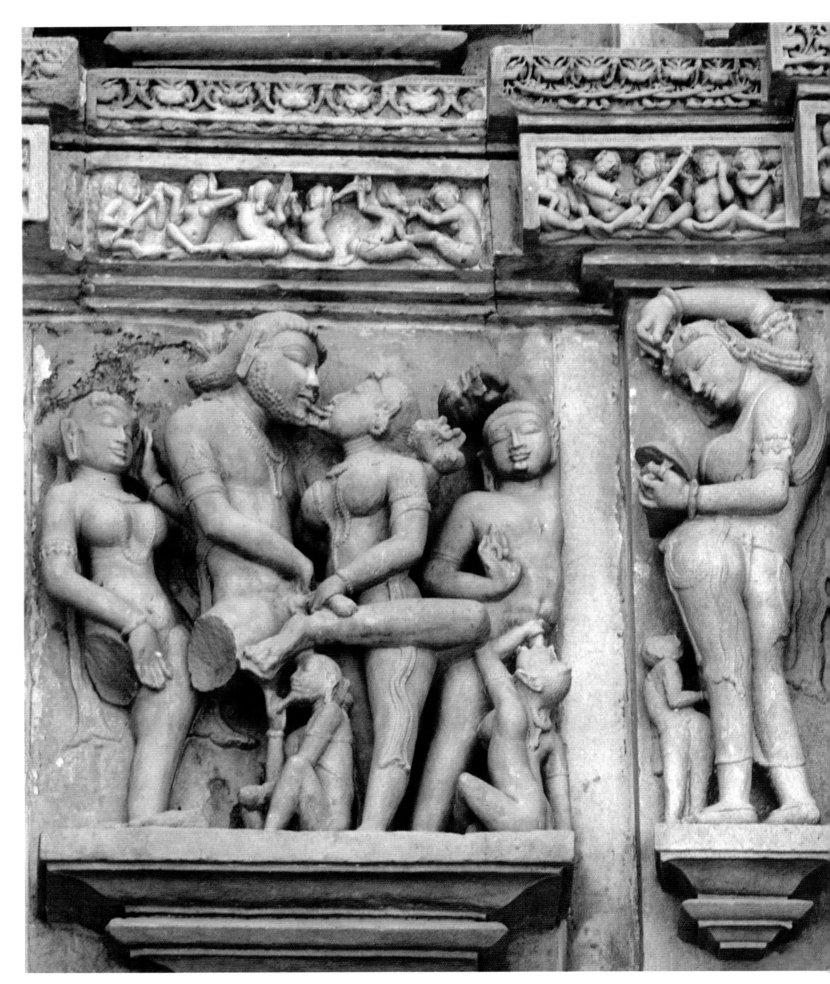

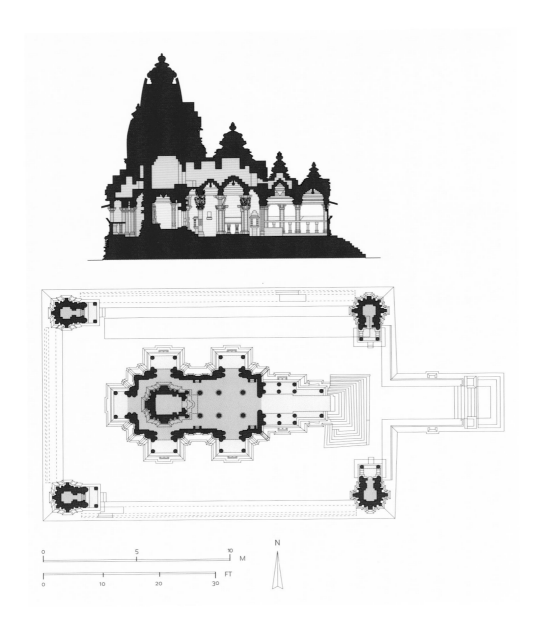

Pages 134–135

Paeans in praise of desire
The scenes that decorate the towers of the Khajuraho temples exalt the language of love and carnal attraction. To the left, lovers (*mithunas*) give themselves to their passions. In the centre, a four-armed god is flanked by two gracious *apsaras*; one contemplates her reflection in a mirror, the other holds a lotus flower. Right, a couple is entertained by the antics of a little monkey. A string course on the main frieze shows a variety of erotic positions.

The Lakshmana Temple at Khajuraho
Longitudinal section and plan of the temple of Lakshmana at Khajuraho, founded in 954. Surrounded by its four temples, the Lakshmana Temple has a vestibule preceding a space in the form of a double cross. This is created by the five projecting verandas, four lateral and one at the back.

Ingenious Innovations in Layout

The Lakshmana Temple was a turning point. From that time on, the formula prevailing in Bhubaneshwar, for example in the Lingaraja Temple, with its arbitrary juxtaposition of separate elements, was abandoned. In its place came a unitary conception of the temple. At Khajuraho, the classical temples exhibit a fusion of the separate elements that is wholly original.

This aim is clearly to be seen in the Kandariya Mahadeva Temple. It seems to have been built in the reign of Vidyadhara (1017–1029) and represents the apogee of Indian medieval architecture.

The body of the building is raised on a platform 4 m high. The temple itself is some 22 m long and 12.5 m wide, if we exclude the balconies and verandas that project laterally and extend the 'apse' end. The tower is 32 m high. A large axial staircase giving access to the platform leads to the square entrance, with its two pillars on either side; the sides of the entrance are open above a parapet wall. Then comes the oblong *ardha mandapa*, or vestibule, whose roof is supported by eight pillars.

The visitor has now reached the outer limit of the temple proper, as defined by *mandapa* and *shikhara*, and passes through a narrow passage in the transverse wall into the first square *mandapa* or dance pavilion. With its heavily carved roof

The dark interior of the Lakshmana

The southern section of the circumambulatory corridor that surrounds the *garbha griha* in the tenth-century Lakshmana Temple in Khajuraho. It is dimly lit by one of the lateral verandas. Right, the reliefs surrounding the entrance to the sanctum (*garbha griha*).

Below left

The divine image in the Lakshmana Temple

In the depths of the *garbha griha* of the Lakshmana Temple the divine image of Vishnu awaits sacrifice and the offerings of the devotee. The hieratic, frontal sculpture is a powerful expression of Vishnu's majesty.

Below right

The dwelling of the god in the Lakshmana Temple

The mysterious atmosphere of the inner sanctuary is well demonstrated in the Lakshmana Temple, where the pillars of the *mandapa* create a distant perspective into the *garbha griha*.

Side view of the Chitragupta Temple at Khajuraho, dedicated to Surya, the god of the sun. Constructed *circa* 1000, it lacks the vertical thrust of the Kandariya Mahadeva Temple. But the various architectural elements are arranged in similar fashion, despite the fact that the Chitragupta Temple has only one pair of lateral verandas. It also lacks a circumambulatory corridor.

A temple entrance: the Kandariya Mahadeva Temple

The vestibule of the Kandariya Mahadeva Temple at Khajuraho. Access is through an ornate portal with a multi-lobed false arch under a projecting roof. Above it rises the finely sculpted roof of the *ardha-mandapa*. Further back along the axis rises the tower, crowned by the fluted disk of the *amalaka*.

Page 138 below
The Devi Jagadamba Temple at Khajuraho

The Devi Jagadamba Temple at Khajuraho, dedicated first to Vishnu, then to Kali, also lacks a circumambulatory corridor. The temple dates from the late eleventh century and has sculpted decoration of superlative quality.

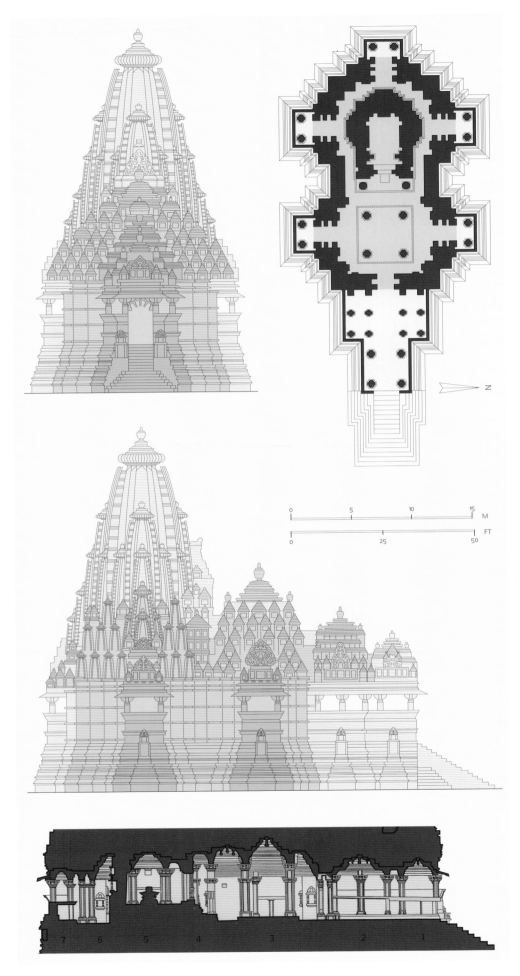

The paradigm of perfection
Elevation of the façade, plan, side elevation and section of the accessible spaces of the Kandariya Mahadeva Temple at Khajuraho. The temple was built by King Vidyadhara (1017–1029) of the Chandella dynasty. In this temple, the integration of the different spaces attains its maximum coherence. The *mandapa, garbha griha* and circumambulatory corridor form a single space lit by the five verandas and the vestibule (*ardha-mandapa*). The section shows the extraordinary quantity of solid masonry relative to the small internal spaces.

1 *Ardha-mandapa*
2 *Mandapa*
3 *Maha-mandapa*
4 *Antarala*
5 *Garbha griha*
6 *Pradakshinapatha*
7 Axial balcony

**The surging 'spires' of the
Kandariya Mahadeva Temple**
In silhouette resembling a veritable cathedral of the Middle Ages, the Kandariya Mahadeva Temple at Khajuraho raises its pyramidal roofs into the sky, culminating in the *shikhara*. The tower is surrounded by smaller buttressing turrets. In the early eleventh century, while still devoid of arch and vault, the architecture of medieval India attained something very close to perfection.

Structural and ornamental
cohesion: the Kandariya
Mahadeva Temple
The verandas of the Kandariya
Mahedeva Temple at Khajuraho
allow light into the interior as
well as forming lateral and axial
buttresses; but also lighten the
structure by needing only columns
to support their overhanging roof.

supported by four pillars, it is relatively dark; light enters from the entrance passage
and from the bays on either side that lead to projecting verandas. The roof-structure of the verandas is supported by two pillars, and their transverse projection
emphasises the cruciform plan of the *mandapa*.

Behind the *mandapa*, two more pillars precede the *cella*, within which the *garbha
griha* or sanctum presents an axial opening. It is a bare cell measuring a mere 2.5 by
3 m and it contains the linga of Shiva. Situated beneath the *shikhara*, the *cella* stands
within a solid mass of masonry occupying the centre of the temple.

Around the *cella* is a narrow corridor forming a kind of ambulatory. This provides
space for the rite of circumambulation, which is performed clockwise. On either
side of the sanctum, projecting verandas look out over the landscape. They form
another transverse axis, as in the *mandapa*; a fifth veranda terminates the apse.

This part of the temple set below the *shikhara* is very dark. The verandas on the
three sides of the apse allow some light into the ambulatory; but in the *cella*, the
mystery of the *garbha griha* remains enveloped in darkness – except when, on certain days of the year, the rays of the rising sun strike, as if to wake the image of the
deity from its slumbers.

The plan of the Kandariya Mahadeva Temple is typical of a number of the Khajuraho temples. It performs the double task of unifying the building as a whole, while
respecting its component parts.

Under the influence of an anonymous architect of undoubted genius, the Hindu
temple ceased to be a series of juxtaposed elements and formed instead an organic
unity; the various components – vestibule, dance pavilion, sanctum and ambulatory
– are brought within a single, unified system. So there is now a spatial continuum.

This 'Lorraine cross' plan, articulated around an axial entrance and five identical
verandas, results in a symmetry and repetition characteristic of Hindu architectural

The mystical light of the Kandariya
Mahadeva Temple
The dim light within the Shivaite
Kandariya Mahadeva Temple
comes from the lateral verandas
whose four columns bear the
lintels on which the stone beams
of the roof-structure are carried.
These pillars support brackets surmounted by capitals. The brackets
are mostly decorated with supporting figures, though many
of them have unfortunately disappeared.

The structure of the Kandariya Mahadeva Temple's west end
The west end of the Temple at Khajuraho has a veranda within a rigorously symmetrical structure. At the base of the tower, deeply carved mouldings impart visual stability. Then come sculpted friezes that run around the projections and re-entrants of the temple walls. Finally, miniature turrets buttress the *shikhara*.

A broad opening in the Kandariya Mahadeva Temple
Seen from the southern veranda, the *ardha-mandapa* of the Kandariya Mahadeva Temple at Khajuraho resembles a balcony with a forest of pillars supporting the roof. The *ardha-mandapa* is flooded with light and forms a transition between the vestibule and the darkness of the great *mandapa*.

thinking. The verandas are all of identical structure in plan and elevation. They impart a rhythm to the mass of the building, which in plan presents, from the entrance westwards, a series of stepped projections culminating in the first set of verandas, after which it narrows through an identical series of stepped recessions, before widening again towards the second set of verandas. The series of symmetrical recessions preceding the second pair of verandas is exactly reproduced by the back; in consequence, the series of recessions is identical on both east–west and north–south axes. At Khajuraho, the coherence and rigour of the plan are still further refined.

Vertical Organisation

It is the *shikhara* that governs the vertical organisation of the Khajuraho temples. This can be seen all the more clearly now that these buildings present a real unity.

In the Kandariya Mahadeva Temple, a succession of elements accentuates the skyward dynamic. Not only do the pyramidal roofs of the entrance, vestibule and *mandapa* constitute a series, with each higher than the last, but the tower itself also contains within itself horizontal and vertical registers that serve to emphasise its soaring height.

The base of the temple itself also contributes to this upward movement through a series of horizontal mouldings consisting of some thirty large and small concave mouldings set one on top of another. To accentuate the impression of stability, the lower part of the base is wider than the upper, as if it had been broadened by impact with the ground. The layers of deep horizontal grooves running around the plinth powerfully reassert the balance of the building as a whole.

A second level is constituted by the façades at the base of the tower, where the ornamental sculpture is profuse. This is a point of equilibrium, a moment of repose

The tower rises like the jets of a fountain
The tower of the Kandariya Mahadeva Temple attains 40 m in height, rising in a single upward movement in which the convergent smaller turrets buttress the central *shikhara*. The pattern of repeated motifs (*candrashalas*) covers the *rekha deul*; they represent the dwellings of the divine city.

Structural organisation of the Kandariya Mahadeva Temple
The lower part of the tower of the Kandariya Mahadeva Temple is marked by a series of strong horizontal mouldings. Above them is the triple register of sculpted friezes running around the projections of the outer wall of the *cella*. They, in their turn, underpin the vigorous upward surge of the miniature towers. The composition of these elements gives structure to the upward movement of the building.

in which the decoration can be contemplated; it possesses its own rhythm, one created by the intersection of the deep vertical grooves and the pronounced horizontal entablatures. In the play of projection and recession making up the sculpted surfaces, the tendency towards the vertical is already affirmed. This section is capped by a cornice marking the division between the walls of the temple and its roof.

A third level is constituted by the roof of the temple. It is the standard Nagara formula, with the surging convex volumes of the turrets forming the *shikhara*. They seem to spring upward from the cornice and are themselves composed of diminutive *shikharas*, towers built to a much smaller scale, whose stepped proliferation reproduces the principal ornamental motif, that of the *candrashala*, with the wheel of the sun or *amalaka* at its summit and the *kalasha* vase above that.

All these structures, from the smallest to the largest, buttress one another and lead the eye up to the culminating point. The ascent is an explosion of mutually reinforcing shapes, a jostling intricacy of verticals and parabolas. Andreas Volwahsen counted some eighty-four turrets on the main *shikhara*.

The principal tower of the temple unites all these apparently disparate elements into a single unit, surging rocket-like into the heavens.

In front of the *shikhara*, the roof-structures of the *mandapa* and *ardha-mandapa* rise in steps, along which are aligned miniature edifices. The successive gradations of steps reflect their corbelled structure and form pyramids in the classic Nagara style. These roofs symbolise the residence of the gods on Mount Meru.

The Meaning of the 'Erotic' Decoration

The sculpture on the walls of the temples at Khajuraho displays a fantastic variety of scenes that would, in the earlier twentieth century, have been considered licentious, if not actually pornographic. The erotic component of this theme – erotic in the proper sense of evoking sensual love – first shocked, then attracted. The motives underlying this attraction were not always artistic; they sometimes sought to justify liberation and excess of all kinds. We need to seek the profounder meaning of the hymn to carnal love that covers the most beautiful temples of Khajuraho.

These scenes are not isolated, hidden away from the believer, such as are those found in the inner chambers of the brothels in Pompeii and Herculaneum. On the contrary, the erotic theme is a *leitmotif* in certain parts of the façades of the sanctuaries.

There is no concealment. The embracing couples are exhibited alongside the gods of the Hindu pantheon. Without thought of modesty or offence, the sculptors have focused on the act of coitus. The sculptures constitute a paean of praise to the sexual act in its most complex forms. As a result, the refinement of the poses and their very ostentation confer on them a kind of nobility. There is nothing remotely vulgar about these works.

This description does not do justice to the artistry of the sculptures, which are among the masterpieces of Indian art. But it is their presence on places of worship that we have to account for. In Hindu mythology, divine perfection consists in unity. The separation of masculine and feminine in the natural world creates a tension, the desire to unite and create in the manner of the gods. Serenity results from the union of complementary opposites.

Since the source of all terrestrial existence lies in this masculine–feminine opposition, their conjunction symbolises the creative act. The modalities of this act, which is akin to the original act of Creation, are symbolised in Shivaism by the union of male and female principles, represented by the linga (the phallus as symbol of the Creator, Shiva) and the *yoni* (the vulva as symbol of the mother-goddess, Shakti, whose daughter Parvati is Shiva's wife).

The geometry of the *yantras*
The participants disporting themselves amorously on the façade of the Kandariya Mahadeva Temple at Khajuraho form a very expert geometry. The postures of the central group, a man and three women, here create a hexagonal pattern constituting a *yantra*. Based on the mystic Tantra, this erotic discipline is part of a quest for the sources of life and procreation in the Hindu mythological universe.

The modalities of the sexual act – the positions of sexual union – are not merely recapitulations of the voluptuous, but manifestations also of procreation in all its diversity. Art affirms the presence of the Great Law (*dharma*), founded on the perpetuation of life, in the cycle of creation and destruction represented by Shiva's cosmic dance.

This law discovers in erotic variation a sensuality poles away from the simple act of copulation. Here, imagination presides over the erotic act. Through it, desire seeks expression. Imagination allows sexual pleasure to be magnified, lending to love its true cosmic dimension. Thus art transcends and transfigures nature, making the sexual act also a mystic and ritual act. At Khajuraho we witness the staging of the sexual act in a ceremonial context that sacralises the gestures of the amorous couples (*mithunas*).

The exercise of erotic powers is subject to the symbolism of creation myths, through which humans participate in the divine. The magical game of love must be considered in the tradition of the Tantra, a philosophical doctrine concerning certain ritual practices, which are not accepted in orthodox cults. In tantric thought, the realisation of the individual is accomplished through physical disciplines (*sadhanas*) related to yoga. Based on the symbolic encounter of female and male energy, the tantric exercise is intended to lead to unity, and unity rediscovered is the source of all wisdom.

Laughter or modesty?
Should we read embarrassment or amusement in the gesture of this celestial nymph, who hides her face at the scenes depicted on the façade of the Kandariya Mahadeva Temple?

The massed proselytes of love
The three registers of friezes on the tower of the Kandariya Mahadeva Temple at Khajuraho are somewhat reminiscent of the saints and kings found in the porches of medieval cathedrals in the West. On closer examination, the theme here is rather different, even if the exaltation of divine power is analogous. Here the combination of the *apsaras*, images of Shiva and the interlocked bodies practising 'divine eroticism' create a veritable hymn to life.

The splendours of the
celestial city
On the front of the temples, the
games of love set the god Shiva
among seductive nymphs and
amorous couples (*mithunas*).
To the right, a *surasundari*
beneath palm-branches evokes
the beauties of nature.

An Initiatory Language

To illustrate the 'staging' of the erotic in the sculptures of Khajuraho, let us consider the several individuals who sometimes participate in a single sexual act. The arrangement of their bodies and their postures are sometimes governed by the symmetrical requirements of the *mandala*. The composition as a whole then takes on geometrical form (triangle, hexagon, octagon or other) and thus refers back to the architectural plan, which we have already considered.

It is especially notable that this representational pattern is very often found surmounting the narrow passage that separates the large entrance hall (*mandapa*) from the inner sanctum proper. At this meeting point between the *garbha griha*, the world of the gods, and the profane world (which extends up to and includes the temple's entrance hall), a short encounter between the ritually depicted god and the believer takes place. Two otherwise separate worlds meet for a brief period of time, and this is symbolised by the bodily union depicted in erotic imagery.

It is therefore no surprise that naturalism is effectively absent from the sculptures. This is a highly stylised art that seeks in abstract form an ideal of beauty to which it constantly returns. The figures portrayed are long and slender, the women broad-hipped, with slim waists and high, round breasts. No muscles are delineated in the round, tapering legs. The faces of both sexes are angular, with finely cut profiles. Their gaze is suggested by long, slanting eyes beneath arched eyebrows; their noses are straight or slightly aquiline, and their mouths are clearly defined but not fleshy.

Such are these idealised figures who, in their aspiration to serenity, participate in a feast of the senses the better to sublimate their desire in a mystical transfiguration of the gestures of love. In this perspective, the source of pleasure, the sexual act, is seen to correspond to the laws of the universe. The devotee looking at the sculptures understands that the accomplishment of the self on the physical plane is a source of *kama* or pleasure. But this liberation of being by self-realisation leads to a maturing of the individual on the spiritual plane and thus offers access to the insights of the *dharma*, the gaining of religious merit through following the Sacred Law.

For this reason, the sculptures of Khajuraho have only the appearance of eroticism, at least in the usual sense of the term. They illustrate a spirituality that confers a cosmic dimension on the sexual act by harmonising it with the rhythms of the universe. The *mithunas* on the walls of the temples illustrate this teaching, while the beautiful nymphs serve as expressions of the beauty of the world.

Under the eye of the *apsaras*
The scenes on the façade of the
Kandariya Mahadeva Temple show
groups forming intricate sexual
patterns and evoke a sensual
refinement far from vulgarity or
obscenity. In them we perceive
the aspiration to be dissolved in
universal harmony.

Unity at Nagda
The main temple at Nagda presents a curvilinear tower and a substantial hypostyle pavilion (*mandapa*). It combines in a single room vestibule, *mandapa* and lateral verandas. A single pyramidal roof covers this space.

The Jain Temples of Rajasthan and Gujarat

While Hindu art was reaching its greatest heights at Khajuraho, where the few Jain temples are barely distinguishable from the Hindu sanctuaries, the Jain religion was expanding. The result was a series of buildings dating from the eleventh to the fourteenth centuries. The devotees of Mahavira adopted Hindu forms – even down to the beautiful nymphs and *mithunas* described above – and showed their prosperity by building all or part of their temples in magnificent materials, such as the white marble famously used in the temple at Mount Abu. At great expense, they had the blocks of stone required for their temples transported to the temple sites. The quality of this superlative material allowed the sculptors to give their full measure in meticulously detailed work. Pillars, sculptures and decorative work were carved as though in ivory.

The Temples of Sasbahu, at Nagda, date from the late tenth century. They are relatively modest in scale and conform to the general outlines of the Nagara style; they are somewhat reminiscent of Khajuraho.

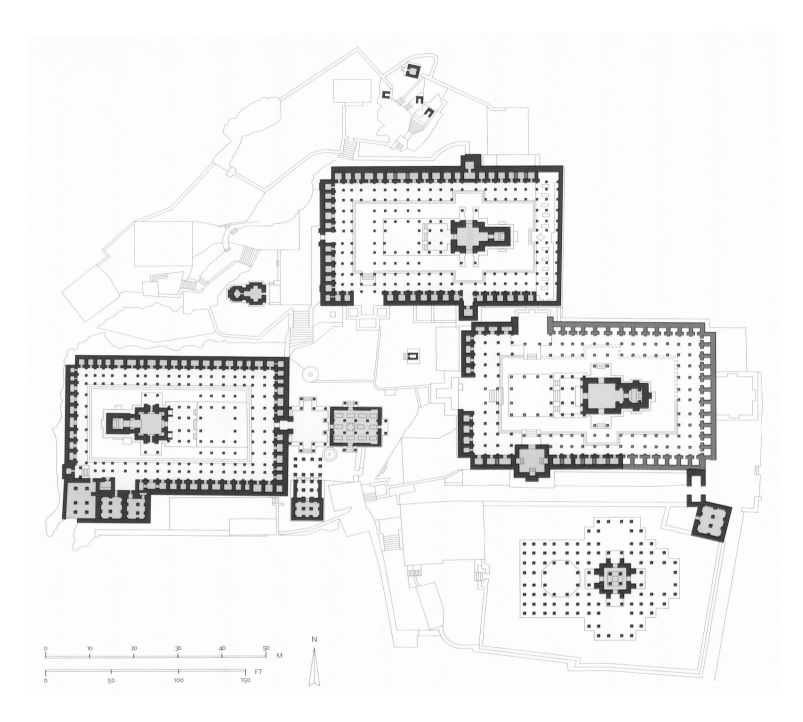

0 10 20 30 40 50 M

0 50 100 150 FT

N

Mount Abu: a Jain holy city

The four Jain temples of Mount Abu in South Rajasthan are all of similar plan and form a complex celebrated for the quality of its sculpture. From left to right: the Vimala Vasahi Temple, dedicated to Adinatha, built between 1032 and 1045; the Luna Vasahi or Neminatha Temple, dating from 1230; and a second temple dedicated to Adinatha. Around these three temples are walls lined with cells. Finally, the Parshvanatha Temple (bottom right).

Page 155

An early masterpiece: the Vimala Vasahi

The entrance of the Jain Temple of Vimala Vasahi at Mount Abu has a false dome resting on finely wrought supports. It leads into an octagonal *mandapa*, whose pillars support a prodigious corbelled 'dome' decorated with sixteen celestial nymphs. All the lintels are reinforced by brackets, using an ingenious system of triangulated supports that compensates for the lack of arches.

Page 156 above

**A corbelled dome in the
Luna Vasahi**

The Luna Vasahi or Neminatha
Temple at Mount Abu dates from
1230 and has a superlative false
dome decorated with swarms
of delicately carved divinities.
The virtuosity of the sculptors is
particularly evident in the sixteen
celestial nymphs.

Page 156 below

**The triumph of ornament in
the Vimala Vasahi Temple**

The system of triangulated supports with their sinuous brackets
allowed the Jain architects to
dispense with the arch. These
exquisite perforated garlands
first appeared at Mount Abu in
the Jain temple of Vimala Vasahi
in the eleventh century.

**Dominating the temple
at Ranakpur**

Balconies buttress the central
tower of the great Jain temple at
Ranakpur dedicated to Adinatha.
The temple is surrounded by porticoed courtyards and dates from
1439.

One of the *mandapas*, probably a later addition, presents intricately carved pillars; it also possesses what Auguste Choisy calls the 'triangulated timber-frame
style' that allows the thrust of flat corbelled 'domes' to be absorbed.

From the eleventh century on, the isolated site of Mount Abu, hidden away in the
Aravalli hills in southern Rajasthan, became one of the main pilgrimage centres for
Jain devotees. The temples of Dilwara and, even more so, the Vimala Vasahi Temple
(1032) dedicated to Adinatha, and the Luna Vasahi Temple (*circa* 1230) dedicated to
Neminatha, exhibit a profusion of exquisitely detailed ornament.

The false dome of the sanctuary rests on an octagonal base and comprises eight
pillars joined by false arches and their triangulated braces, reinforced by brackets.
This formula was maintained as late as the sixteenth century, in defiance of the by
then familiar technique of the arch. The false dome technique is itself virtuosic, and
Jain architects showed a perfect mastery of its construction and ornamentation;
divinities abound in the carvings.

A prodigious mastery of the false dome: Ranakpur

The immense Jain temple at Ranakpur, dedicated to Adinatha in 1439, includes superlative internal spaces. Its corbelled 'domes', built in white marble, rest on octagonal bases and make use of a sophisticated system of lintels on columns. Coffered ceilings occupy the space around the octagon.

The lightness and elegance of Ranakpur

The prolific ornament of the Jain temple at Ranakpur provided the sculptors of the fifteenth century with a challenge to their virtuosity. Not a single surface escapes the sculptors' attention. The gloom traditional in temple interiors has given way to floods of light that reach every part of the building.

A forest of columns at Ranakpur
The assembly room in the great
Temple of Adinatha at Ranakpur
gives the impression of a maze of
infinite extent. The visitor to
these hypostyle halls and courtyards alternating with corbel-
domed spaces receives an overwhelming impression of freedom
and serenity. The architecture of
India is transfigured: mystic gloom
gives way to illumination.

**A rigorous organisation of space
at Ranakpur**
Based on the square, the plan of
the Adinatha Temple at Ranakpur
(1439) is in fact essentially cruciform. The central temple has four
secondary *cellae* around it, forming a group of five and there are
twenty corbelled false domes
arranged in groups of five on the
axes of the building.

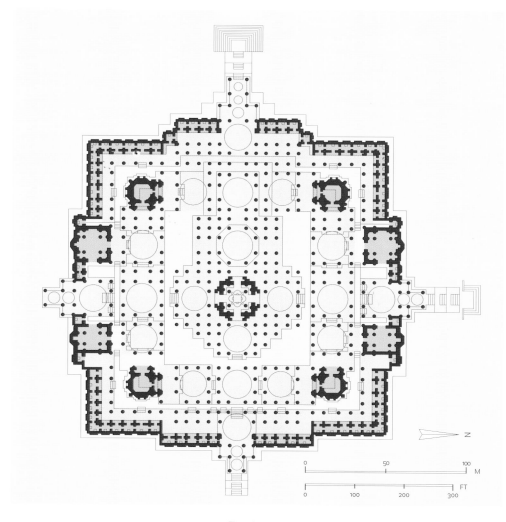

The Surya Temple at Ranakpur
This temple, dedicated to the Sun God, was probably built in the thirteenth century and was restored in the fifteenth century after its sacking by Muslim invaders heading for Gujarat. Its *mandapa* is octagonal and has six verandas. The east side of the octagon opens on to the vestibule and the west side on to the sanctum.

The end of the Surya Temple at Ranakpur
Sculpted in superb white limestone, the end of the temple shows the Sun God seated with the characteristic lotus blossoms; below, a part of the horse frieze, which runs around the whole temple, alluding to the solar chariot.

Page 161
Intricate ornament at Ranakpur
At the entrance to the sanctum of the Surya Temple, the intricately wrought columns with lathe-turned capitals support intersecting corbels carved with benevolent gnomes. The technique of triangulated supports, with projecting, sinuous brackets, reached a peak of sophistication at Ranakpur.

**The Neminatha Temple
at Ranakpur**
The Neminatha Temple at
Ranakpur is dedicated to
Tirthankara, 'he who made the
crossing possible', and dates from
the fifteenth century. This handsome Jain temple allows the tide
of ornament to wash unopposed
over the entire building, from the
base to the summit of its Nagara-
style tower.

**Exaltation of the dance on
the Neminatha Temple**
Detail of one of the *apsaras* –
musicians and dancers – who
inhabit the divine city depicted
on the temple. Jewellery and
other trappings are now among
the principal features of these
celestial nymphs.

**The relief ornament of the
Neminatha Temple**
Strictly ordered in superimposed
registers, the ornament of the
Neminatha Temple combines
fifteenth-century relief carvings
on the recently restored tower,
left, with those of a *mandapa*.

The high podium of the Jagadisha Temple at Udaipur
The Jagadisha Temple at Udaipur dates from 1651. The stiff treatment of its pillared *mandapa* is typical of later temple building.

The Jagadisha Temple tank in Udaipur
The huge ablution tank at the Jagadisha Temple in Udaipur is sunk deep into the earth. A series of symmetrical flights of stairs allows the faithful to descend into its well.

Pages 164–165

A fabulous holy city: Palitana
The city of Palitana in Gujarat was destroyed by the Muslim invaders and entirely restored in the sixteenth and seventeenth centuries. It contains 836 Jain temples. Its temples to Adinatha and Tirthankara form a sacred city entirely given over to meditation.

Proof of this mastery is found not only at Mount Abu but in the fabulous halls of the Jain Temple of Adinatha at Ranakpur. This was built by the architect Depaka in 1439. It is an immense complex, with its halls, shrines, passages, towers with superposed verandas, perforated columns and lintels overflowing with figures and decorative motifs. It is, in short, a masterpiece.

Further south, in the state of Gujarat, the vast Jain Complex at Palitana covers the upper levels of a mountain, and comprises no fewer than 836 sanctuaries and shrines. This extraordinary ensemble was begun in the eleventh century, but was entirely reconstructed by the followers of Jain after the destruction perpetrated in the fourteenth and fifteenth centuries by the Muslims. Of what survives, nothing is earlier than the sixteenth century. The forms present here are very similar to those already encountered at Mount Abu and at Nagda.

In the same period, in the Udaipur-Chitorgarh region, Vaishnavite temples were also being reconstructed. The sanctuary of Jagadisha was built in 1651. It combines a kind of hypostyle *mandapa* with a large tank, the many staircases of which allow the devotee access to the water even when the level is very low.

NEW ARCHITECTURE IN THE DECCAN

The Hoysala Style and the 'Soapstone' Temples

Page 167

The jostling crowds of the friezes
At the dawn of the second millennium, architecture in southern India saw the development of an extraordinarily rich system of sculpted decoration. Everywhere we see divinities, processions, scenes of war and parades of victory. Compared with the large-scale statuary of Khajuraho, much of this work is rather small. This relief from the Keshava Temple at Somnathpur showing multitudes surrounding a four-wheeled cart is like a miniature cartoon strip, full of action and animation.

The Hoysala style
The Hoysala dynasty (eleventh–fourteenth centuries) reigned over the region of today's Mysore. One of the characteristics of Hoysala statuary is the dark steatite from which it is sculpted; its fine grain allows the material to be carved like a precious stone. This seated Ganesha from the temple of Halebid is typical. The elephant-headed god wears a most elaborate helmet and head-dress and carries the symbol of his father's power, the axe of Shiva.

Our first tour of Hindu architecture has taken us on a wide swing through Ellora, Elephanta and Badami via Aihole and Pattadakal, to Thanjavur in the south, and thence to Bhubaneshwar and Konarak in the north-west. From there we visited Khajuraho in the north and Mount Abu in the west. Now it is time to return to the south and speak of the Hoysala kingdom. Centred on Mysore in the state of Karnataka, it was between the eleventh and early fourteenth century a vigorous independent kingdom of the Dravidian south.

The Hoysala dynasty lasted from 1020 to 1342. It was contemporary with the Ganga dynasty in Orissa, the Chalukyas of Kalyani (who had succeeded the Chalukyas of Badami), the Chandellas of Khajuraho, and the decline of the Cholas of Thanjavur; so that it represents an original and fecund transition between the last of the Chalukyas and the future kingdom of the Vijayanagaras (1336–1586), which was to be the last Hindu bastion against the Muslim invaders.

The Hoysala dynasty extended its power throughout southern India, covering a region extending from Mamallapuram and Kanchipuram in the east to what is now the state of Kerala in the west. The Hoysalas were originally Jains, but they later turned to Hinduism and set about building a series of sumptuous temples. We shall concentrate on three representative sites: Halebid, Belur and Somnathpur. Some of the temples there are among the most remarkable monuments of the period.

In 1117, the Hoysala king Bittideva, who had taken the name Vishnuvardhana to mark his devotion to Vishnu, founded the Chennakeshava Temple at Belur to celebrate an important victory over the Cholas of Thanjavur. About the same time, the dynastic Hoysaleshvara Temple began to be built at Halebid, along with a Jain temple, the Parshvanatha Temple. (Halebid is the Muslim name for the former capital, Dvarasamudra, and means 'Old Capital'.) Finally, the construction of the Keshava Temple at Somnathpur marked the culmination of the Hoysala style.

In 1327, the Hoysala kingdom was submerged in the wave of Islamic invasions. It was soon afterwards liberated by the neighbouring Hindu kingdom of Vijayanagara, which arose about the year 1336 in the Hampi region. In 1397, a Vijayanagara general commemorated the expulsion of the Muslims from Belur by setting up a *gopuram* at the entrance to the Chennakeshava Temple.

Among the other architectural achievements of this period, particular note should be taken of the Lakshmidevi Temple at Dodda Gaddavalli, whose construction began in 1112, in the reign of the Hoysala King Vishnuvardhana; the Temple of Balleshvara at Arsikere, which dates from 1220; and the Lakshmi Narasimha Temple at Nugginalli, built about 1249; all of them near Hassan; and of the temples of Balagamve near Shimoga (notably the Kedareshvara Temple).

The Style of the Hoysala Temples

The Hoysala dynasty gave rise to a very individual style of Hindu and Jain temple, in the opinion of some historians equivalent to the Vesara, or 'hybrid', style, since it lies half-way between the Nagara and the Dravidian styles. It is immediately distinguishable from the other architectural productions of medieval India by its highly original star plans and by the profusion of refined sculptures and reliefs carved into the superb dark steatite stone.

One characteristic frequently ascribed to the Hoysala style is its structural horizontality. This is unjust; the temples of which this is said are either incomplete or damaged. Though Hoysala towers were not of the highest, the lack or removal of the pyramidal roof-structure and of the upper part of the tower necessarily affects the profile of the whole temple.

A feature truly characteristic of the Hoysala temples is the use of finely worked mouldings on the columns, which are made with the use of a lathe, as we saw with the latest temples of the Badami Chalukyas. The columns are turned like balusters, using techniques developed for woodworking, and this gives them a profile like that of a spinning top. The contrasting cylindrical projections and grooves make the columns look like stacks of plates.

The plans of the Hoysala style of temple display a preoccupation with spatial unity such as we have already seen at Khajuraho. The temple is no longer a series of juxtaposed units (ardha-mandapa + mandapa + shikhara), but the result of a programme intended to unify the various functions of the temple into an organic whole.

A new concept was arrived at, which is exemplified by the Chennakeshava Temple at Belur. It has a high platform with many projections and re-entrants that forms a wide terrace around the temple, thus facilitating the rite of circumambulation and allowing the sculptures to be admired from close-to. On the platform, the temple presents a double cruciform structure.

The huge dance pavilion and meeting hall consists of a hypostyle hall with three entrances at three cardinal points; the entrance to the sanctuary is at the fourth. There are altogether forty-six columns, whose arrangement is dictated by the central crossing. The external walls are decorated with the stone claustra known as jali. These were installed some fifty years after completion of the building, in the reign of Ballala II.

At one end of this hall, on the central axis, is the tiny cella. It is preceded by a vestibule of the same size, whose roof rests on four columns. But the base of the tower (which is cruciform in plan) is given a dense curtain of masonry that makes the arms of the cross star-shaped. The plan is clearly not dictated by that of the cella. But it does allow the luxurious sculpted ornament to run riot over the external walls, whose zigzag outline presents a greater surface area for relief decoration and statuary. Tower and roof-pyramid are missing; they were demolished in 1880, probably so that their beautiful dark metamorphic schist might be reused.

The great Hoysaleshvara Temple at Halebid is sacred to Nataraja, the dancing Shiva. It is a double building combining two juxtaposed cruciform structures; they communicate on the transverse axis, so that one can move directly between them. The buildings are sacred to Shiva. In each case, the mandapa takes the form of a hypostyle hall. As at Belur, the space between the peripheral columns has been closed off with stone slabs, while there are ten internal columns around the four much larger ones at the centre; the latter delimit a circular area reserved for dancers and musicians.

On the entrance axis, a vestibule leads to the sanctum, the garbha griha. This is of the form that we have already seen in the temple at Belur, but it completes it with three secondary shrines surrounding the central cella and emphasising the cruciform plan. The play of the cuspate projections of solid masonry imparts a stellar outline to each 'apse', an effect enhanced by the profusion of sculpture. This is a

A foretaste of the Vijayanagara style at Belur
Detail of the gopuram leading into the huge (145 by 120 m) precinct of the Chennakeshava Temple at Belur, founded in 1117. The swarming ornamentation typifies the art of the fourteenth century Vijayanagara kingdom, which succeeded the Hoysala dynasty.

Page 171
The monumental gopuram at Belur
The pyramidal gateway at Belur dates from 1397. Its five storeys are crowded with divinities. It was built by a general of the Vijayanagara kingdom at a time when the Hoysala style had already disappeared. But the temple to which it gives access is the Chennakeshava Temple, one of the jewels of twelfth-century south Indian architecture.

The Chennakeshava Temple at Belur
The Chennakeshava Temple at Belur was built in 1117 and is dedicated to Vishnu. Set on a platform whose projections and re-entrants echo the *rathas* of the temple, it now lacks *shikhara* and pyramidal roof-structures.

The rigorous design of the Chennakeshava Temple
The *garbha griha* of the Chennake-shava Temple is clothed in *rathas* like the teeth of a cog-wheel with the result that there is a much larger surface on which the Hoysala sculptors might demonstrate their skill. The orthogonal mouldings frame exquisite carved decoration.

Vivid attention to detail at Belur
These two guardians at the entrance to the Chennakeshava Temple at Belur testify admirably to the dynamism and sweep of twelfth-century Hoysala sculpture. The swirling drapery and dramatic attitudes are brought off dynamically.

A double cross at Belur
A double cruciform plan governs the layout of the Chennakeshava Temple at Belur that dates from 1117. Behind the large hypostyle hall of the *mandapa*, the tower encasing the *garbha griha* has a stellar form. Its original masonry was required to support superstructures that were subsequently demolished.

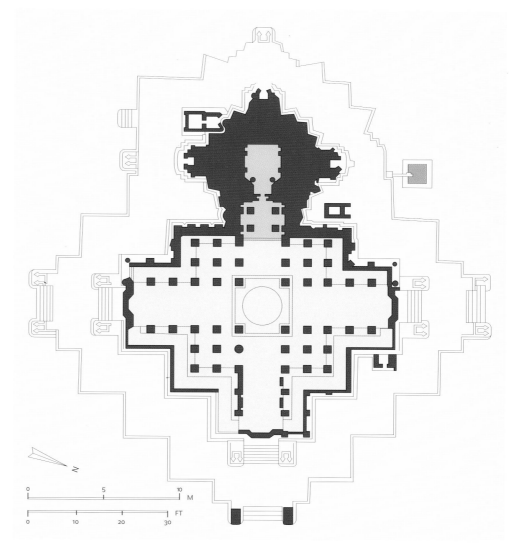

Twin temples at Halebid
Overall view of the double Hoysaleshvara (Lord of the Hoysalas) Temple at Halebid, built in 1150. Like the Chennakeshava Temple at Belur, the temple has been 'decapitated'. The missing *shikharas* clearly affect the appearance of these twin temples, dedicated to Shiva. Their name honours Shiva as master of the Hoysalas. Each is preceded by a pavilion dedicated to the bull Nandi, Shiva's vehicle.

0 5 10 15
M
0 25 50
FT
N

Symmetry at Halebid
Built on a common platform, the double temple of Halebid is rigorously symmetrical in plan except for the two Nandi pavilions that precede the temples. Though each of the two *mandapas* is smaller than that of Belur, in combination they form a huge oblong interior that precedes the two cruciform *garbha grihas*.

The play of horizontals at Halebid
The Hoysaleshvara Temple at Halebid (1150) rises from the ground in superposed registers of friezes. Above them, the *jalis* with which the temple is lined stand between columns turned on the lathe. To the left, the vertical *rathas* in solid masonry mark one of the symmetrical axes of the buildings.

Nine successive levels
The succession of friezes on the base of a Hoysala temple. These generally combine processions of elephants, ornamental mouldings and repeated motifs and run round the entire building, displaying a phenomenal quantity and standard of decorative carving.

Wrought like gold
A procession of gods – Parvati and her *apsaras* in their extravagant finery – covers the end of the Hoysaleshvara Temple at Halebid (1150). Not a single centimetre has escaped the sculptor's chisel.

further development of the star-shaped plan adopted at Belur. These centrally planned interiors should stand under *shikharas*, but only the lower levels of the towers remain, the upper storeys having been destroyed by earthquake.

Where the *mandapa* and *shikhara* join, a mass of masonry projects, its cuspate indentations attracting the eye to this junction and emphasising the unity that it imparts. In the same way, between the *mandapa* and the cella containing the linga, we find powerful buttresses of solid masonry intended to absorb the diagonal thrust of the roof-structure. The pyramidal corbelling has unfortunately been truncated and is now very low.

In front of each of these buildings (which echo each other in almost every respect) stands a little pavilion sacred to the cult of Nandi the bull.

These two temples, with their external colonnades, are set on the same axis as the sanctuaries themselves, but differ in size; the northern pavilion is notably smaller. Both are of similar conception and with their light, airy peristyles composed of turned stone columns, they are clearly designed for the ritual of circumambulation. They both contain an image of Nandi the bull, Shiva's mount. As at Khajuraho, no attempt has been made to integrate these secondary temples and they remain outside the process of architectural unification.

The Perfect Plan of Somnathpur

The stellar plan attains its fullest expression in the Keshava Temple at Somnathpur, built a century later than the temples of Halebid and Belur, in 1268. The central hypostyle hall at Somnathpur comprises internal columns and sixteen peripheral columns linked by *jalis*. Three separate sanctums are each preceded by a vestibule.

This is the formula known as *trikutashala*, and reflects the dedication of the temple to the god Keshava, who represents the three aspects of Vishnu. Each of the cellae displays vigorous projections and re-entrants within and without, and the layout thus created is an emphatically radiating central plan.

These three projecting sanctums are arranged in a cross shape on a stellate terrace, whose outline was obtained by rotating a square 22°30' at a time (360° : 16), so giving rise to a sixteen-point star. If we exclude the platform on which it stands, the temple as a whole is 25 m² and a model of spatial fusion between the *mandapa* as such and the three sanctums, which are axially and elevationally continuous with it. The plan of the Keshava Temple may be said to mark a consummation of the development of medieval Indian architecture.

Protected by an overhanging roof
The entrance of the Hoysaleshvara Temple at Halebid (1150). The stairs lead up to the platform on which the temple is built. On either side are miniature temples, while the *jalis* present their latticework surfaces between columns turned on the lathe.

In the image of the real temple
The two little temples that flank the entrance of the Hoysaleshvara Temple at Halebid give some idea of the original roof-structure of the temple.

The mystic penumbra of the Hoysaleshvara Temple
In the depths of the Hoysaleshvara Temple's *garbha griha*, dim light reveals the linga of Shiva, to which the faithful bring their offerings. The interior of the cella is no less exuberantly decorated than the rest of the temple, built in 1150.

The extent of the Hoysala *mandapa*
Hoysala temples have sizeable internal spaces. The assembly pavilion (*mandapa*) comprises a broad central span supported by four handsome lathe-turned columns, whose capitals carry intersecting corbels on which the architraves rest.

Lantern ceilings
In the hypostyle pavilions of Belur, Halebid and Somnathpur, the roof-structure is still constructed by means of stone beams placed diagonally across the corners of the square. Like the rest of the temple, the ceilings are covered in a dense web of ornamental carving.

The sanctuary stands, moreover, within a magnificent rectangular courtyard 65 by 53 m, in whose walls are smaller individual shrines for pilgrims and ascetics, fourteen of them on the short sides and eighteen on the long. Each cell is covered with a false cupola of the 'lantern cupola' kind, constructed by setting each tier of lintels across the angles of the tier below. The sixty-two cells (8 by 8 m) are similarly vaulted.

In short, in the three examples chosen from Belur, Halebid and Somnathpur, we perceive the successive developments in the plan of the temple. Each tends towards greater architectural coherence. As at Khajuraho, progress is made towards a greater pulling together of the forms and a more perfect conformity of the architecture to ritual requirement. The effect is to unify the entire architectural ensemble and integrate the link between the two main spaces of the temple, the *mandapa* and the cella.

A stellate column
The omnipresent ornament of the Hoysala style places considerable emphasis on the column. Here a multitude of vigorous flutings follows the changing outline of the shaft.

A column of rings
In some Hoysala columns worked on the lathe, projecting rings produce a series of emphatically horizontal mouldings, as though the column were made of stacked cylinders.

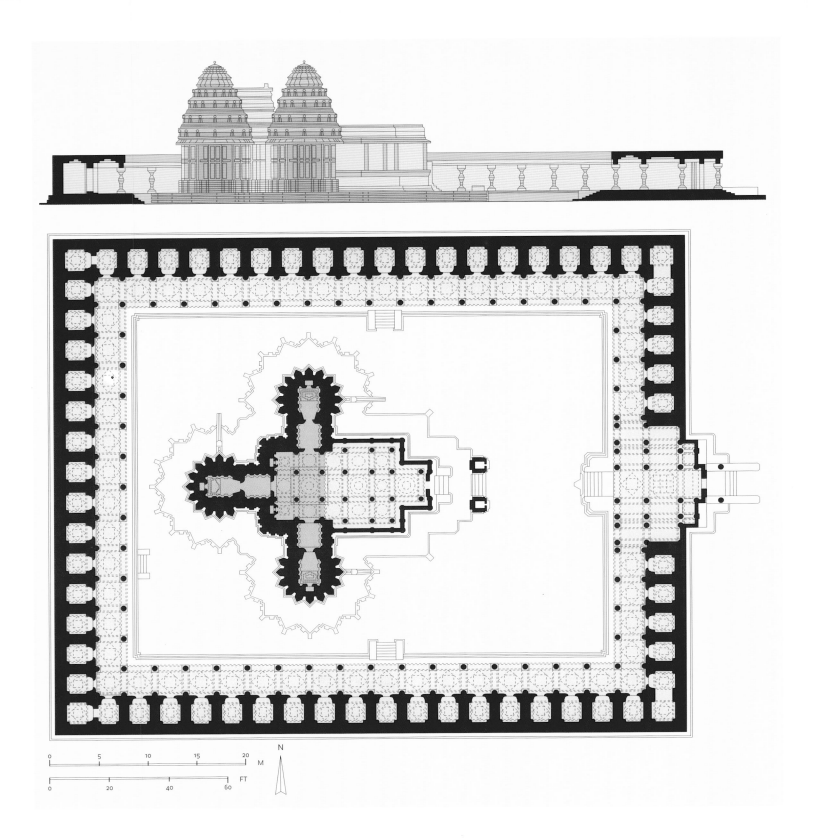

0   5   10   15   20   M

0   20   40   60   FT

N

The design of the Keshava Temple at Somnathpur

Lateral elevation and plan of the Keshava Temple at Somnathpur, near Mysore. Completed in 1268, it is the most perfect of the temples built in the Hoysala style. It lies within a precinct comprising sixty-four cells built to accommodate priests, pilgrims and ascetics. The radiating *rathas* of the three *shikharas* form a stellar plan. The *garbha grihas* are dedicated to Vishnu under his three aspects; this is the meaning of the name Keshava. The hypostyle *mandapa* is very extensive; if we include the external pillars between which latticework *jalis* are fitted, there is a total of thirty-three columns.

The threefold layout of the
Keshava Temple at Somnathpur
Seen from the entrance portal,
the temple at Somnathpur is
rigorously symmetrical, with one
shikhara rising on either side of the
mandapa and a third visible at the
west end of the building.

A Profusion of Sculpture and Decoration

A further distinctive feature of Hoysala temples is the bases, or platforms, on which
they are built. The face of these platforms is carved with deep horizontal mouldings
that emphasise the solid horizontal base on which the temples sit. Some of these
mouldings are continuous and follow the indented plan of the plinth in a sinuous
movement of broken lines. Others are covered in a proliferation of extremely finely
carved reliefs that, like those of the Jain temples of Gujarat and Rajasthan, are reminiscent of ivory carving.

At Belur, the plinth on which the columns and the *jali* of the *claustra* panels stand
is composed of nine successive bands of motifs. The first, at ground level, is formed
by a frieze of elephants, since the elephant was thought to ensure the stability of
the work. Then comes a continuous moulding and, above that, little, stylised *kudu*
motifs.

A fourth level is formed by a highly wrought frieze, comprising a succession of
circles in which minuscule characters are seen performing tiny dramatic scenes.
Above this is a short, repeated motif that projects strongly, like a cornice, and on it
a series of miniature temple 'façades' are juxtaposed on two different registers.

In the gate of each of these miniature temples is carved a deliciously swaying
nymph or a full-face standing divinity. These are clearly further representations of

Mount Meru, the city of the gods. Another strongly projecting cornice is carved like a roof, and on this, somewhat inclined, stands the perimeter wall of the *mandapa*, on which in turn stand the lathe-turned columns and the perforated slabs of the *jali*.

The friezes that run round the perimeter of the building, faithfully modelling each salient of its plan, contain a total of several thousand elephants, several hundred small divinities in their symbolic aedicules and kilometres of repeating decorative motifs.

Either side of the base of the entrance staircase to the temple stand pavilions. They are a kind of small temple with a single miniature cella, surmounted by an elaborated worked pyramidal roof. Sometimes large-scale divinities are found framing such stairs.

At Halebid, the mouldings surrounding the building are still more complex. There are nine registers of friezes, containing elephants, lions, foliated scrolls, processions of horsemen, further scrolls, scenes of everyday life, then strange aquatic monsters amid vegetation, and birds. Above these figurative friezes, the tower is clothed in little upright pieces on which are portrayed divinities, nymphs and goddesses as well as innumerable superlative representations of scenes from Hindu mythology.

These elegant sculptures are executed in steatite with meticulous detail, and their quality leaves one overwhelmed. Armies of sculptors must have collaborated on the immense site to cover the walls of the temple with this multitude of sacred and mythical characters, all exposed to the full light of day and, many of them, figuring in legends known only to the faithful.

The visitor is irresistibly drawn by the magic of the place to wonder at these temples, which are carved like reliquaries in precious metals. Fascinated, one follows the jagged outline of the temples, above which cohorts of gods and goddesses stand, their bodies ornamented with amazingly detailed jewellery and tiaras, and with bracelets and necklaces of endless variety.

Everywhere, the branches and foliage of tropical plant life are translated into stone, linking these figures of artifice to nature and bringing the world of plants, the world of men and the world of gods together in a vast synthesis that emanates an ethereal spirituality.

It would be wrong, however, to consider these works in an exclusively aesthetic light. Whether in the cellae or ornamenting the exterior of the temple, statuary has,

The art of contrasts at Somnathpur
The finely carved friezes and delicate statuary on the walls of the temples at Somnathpur contrast with the almost brutal simplicity of the tank and drain for sacrificial fluids.

in the Hindu religion, a role. This capacity is conferred on it by rites of dedication. In performing the rites by which the statuary was given magical life, the priest first ritually opened the statue's eyes, then bestowed the breath of life on the image of the god. Thereafter, the divine image was inhabited by the god and the temple able to function.

The Creation of Large-scale Internal Spaces

The visitor who enters a Hoysala temple is surprised to find how spacious its halls are, especially when compared with earlier medieval temples. True, the later monuments built by Jain architects, at Ranakpur, for example, and the huge temple-cities of the Nayak (to which we shall return) achieve large-scale internal spaces, and do so despite the lack of arch, vault and dome.

At Halebid, the visitor is able to stroll through the *mandapas* amid the many polished columns, whose shafts glint in the penumbra, and reflect in astonishment on the spaciousness of these halls.

The ceilings are mostly constructed in the 'false lantern dome' style, with stone lintels laid across the corners of the square in order to reduce the span required of the roofing stones. These too are densely carved. In front of the cella door, small-scale temples greet the pilgrim, as if to emphasise the sanctity of the *garbha griha*. The pale light filtering through the *jali* that enclose the assembly hall intensifies this sense of meditation and concentration. And within the sanctum itself, the mystery of cult is hidden beneath the cloak of darkness.

A benevolent deity at the Hoysaleshvara Temple
Ganesha welcomes the visitor to the Hoysaleshvara Temple in Halebid (1150). He is seen seated, as tradition requires, on a large rat. He holds the axe of his father, Shiva, in one hand. Ganesha is a symbol of wisdom and the beloved patron of major enterprises.

Enveloped in finery
This beautiful goddess under the arch formed by a floral interlace decorates a frieze in the Keshava Temple of Somnathpur (thirteenth century). She is a symbol of fecundity or fertility and holds in one hand the lotus, in the other a pine-cone. Her weighty ornaments – diadem, necklace, chain, sacred cord, beaded belt with intricately crafted fringes and anklet – have replaced the nudity usual till then in divinities and celestial nymphs.

The Apotheosis of Southern Indian Architecture

From the Hampi Princes to the Nayaks of Madurai

The last act of the struggle between Hinduism and the Muslim invaders was played out in the kingdoms of southern India. The Islamic conquest inexorably moved towards the south of the Deccan, bringing in its train a wave of iconoclastic destruction. The first incursion of Muhammad of Ghor into the Lahore and Delhi regions dates from 1186. In 1526 came the Mongols with Babur at their head, overwhelming a coalition of Hindu rulers. Akbar strove to create an empire that would cover the whole of northern India and between 1556 and 1605 had succeeded in doing so. By 1707, Aurangzeb ruled over almost the entire peninsula. The Muslim invasion continued irresistibly over a period of five centuries. Only the extreme south, notably Madurai and Thanjavur, escaped Islamic domination.

The Nayak dynasty (1334–1736) saved the south of the Deccan from Muslim conquest. Amid the terrible destruction wreaked by these wars, the Nayaks set about building new, vaster and more exuberant temples in Tamil India, where their reign is associated with a cultural renaissance.

Architectural Developments

The last phase in the development of southern Indian architecture is marked by a huge expansion in the size of temples. From now on, the temple was endowed with a series of strong outer walls, in which the historian perceives a sign of the threat under which the Hindu community lived. The gates were located by enormous *gopurams*, entrance towers of a kind that we have already seen at Thanjavur.

Set at the four cardinal points, the *gopurams* were placed on the succession of walls that soon came to include not just the temple but most of the city also. The accumulation of *gopurams* on the east–west and north–south axes of the city speaks eloquently of the huge built-up areas they were designed to defend; the area within the walls became a veritable temple-city, a formula that found its fullest expression in the vast temples of the Nayak period.

There was consequently a gradual growth in the size of the *gopurams* defending the city, at whose heart the temple lay. The high temple towers (*shikharas*) had previously dominated the town built around the temple; now it was the *gopuram* that became the dominant element.

The temple-cities now perfectly symbolised the divine city surrounded by its mountain ranges (or city walls). They became powerful enclaves within which a society that felt itself beleaguered might seek to ensure the survival of its intense religiosity.

With its concentric systems of walls and axial grid ensuring that the city-temple stood at the centre of the main roads of the town, the city-temple now gained ever higher gates. The further from the *garbha griha* it was, the higher the *gopuram* was built. The result was, paradoxically, that as the symbolic defensive character and sheer scale of its surroundings increased, so the *garbha griha* itself became smaller, thus reversing the previous tendency. The spaces created for meetings and festivities also underwent an enormous increase in scale. The primitive *mandapa* was

replaced by vast hypostyle halls with as many as a thousand pillars, with peripheral porticoes, corridors and immense courtyards. The courtyards stood within inter-locking sets of fortifications. The climax of this process was reached in the sixteenth and seventeenth centuries.

Before considering this final phase, let us look at an older temple at Tiruchirapalli (Trichy). This is the temple dedicated to Venugopala, that is, Krishna, an *avatar* of Vishnu and the flute-playing hero of the *Bhaghavad Gita*. Krishna is here worshipped as the shepherd of souls, while the souls are symbolised as *gopis* (milkmaids).

The Shrirangam Temple at Tiruchirapalli lies on a long island in the middle of the River Kaveri. The charm of Krishna and of his companions the *gopis* is delightfully expressed in the sculptures that decorate the temple. It is a small temple, and forms part of the huge Ranganatha complex. Coeval with Somnathpur, it is built in a very different style; its façades are covered with colonnettes between which miniature temples have been carved. These frame subtle carvings of exquisite feminine divini-ties. One of them, playing the *vina* (a kind of lute), is a discreet allusion to the arts of music and dance in which the divine hero reigns supreme.

Page 193
Architecture with figures: the Venugopala Temple
A detail of the elegant outlines and classical statuary of the Venugopala Temple (1270), now situated within the precinct of the Ranganatha Temple at Tiruchirapalli. A charming *vina* (lute) player is surrounded by evidence of the wood-frame antecedents of this dressed-stone architecture. The capitals to the slender columns echo the tradition of uprights and roof-beams.

The city of Victory

The north *gopuram* of the Pampapati Svami Temple dedicated
to Shiva (Lord of the River). The
temple was built in 1520 at Hampi
by the Vijayanagara dynasty
(1336–1565). Long porticoes
of granite pillars surround the
sanctuary. The city was built in
celebration of a victory over the
Muslims.

The Vijayanagara Dynasty

Hampi, the capital chosen by the generals who in 1336 founded the dynasty of
Vijayanagara ('City of Victory'), occupies an eminently defensible position in a
strange landscape littered with erratic blocks and granite outcrops. Trading in cot-
ton, precious stones and spices made the city immensely prosperous and its warrior
princes were able to construct a whole series of monuments: the Temples of
Vitthala and Krishna, the throne square, the elephant stables, market-places, aque-
ducts and so on. All these were built in the splendid local granite. It was not the most
accommodating medium for stone-carvers, but they demonstrated exceptional virtuosity in its use.

  Hampi finally fell to the victorious Islamic armies in 1565. Sacked during an occu-
pation that lasted six months, the city never recovered. Today, its extensive ruins lie
scattered over many square kilometres.

The lion, an omnipresent symbol
The lion motif at the base of the
pillars of the Pampapati Svami
Temple at Hampi follows a tradition born at Mamallapuram *circa*
500 years earlier.

The great *gopuram* of the Pampapati Svami Temple
The structure of the monumental east gateway of the Pampapati Svami Temple at Hampi is in granite; the ornamental statuary is in whitewashed stucco. Its erotic themes lack the spiritual intensity of Khajuraho's *mithunas*.

The Remains of Hampi

The great Temple of Pampapati Svami – the Master and Lord of the River – is dedicated to an *avatar* of Shiva, though it might more accurately be described as returning to an ancient local cult of the god of the river, who was then assimilated into Shiva.

The temple rises between four *gopurams* standing at the four cardinal points and each of them some fifty metres high. The first of them, on the east or entrance side, has nine storeys, and forms an axial gateway to the complex. Its receding storeys are set on a sturdy granite base and form an oblong pyramid or trapezoid, while its sculptures represent the inhabitants of the celestial domain, the latter evoked by the many miniature temples of the successive storeys.

The four pyramidal *gopurams* with their rectilinear roof-ridges constitute the gates of the first curtain wall of the complex. Their sculpted decoration is framed by rows of colonnettes and is made of stucco. It lacks the imposing elegance of

Architectural ornament at Hampi
This ornamental granite frieze is
from the early sixteenth-century
Vitthala Temple in Hampi and
represents horses and stable boys.

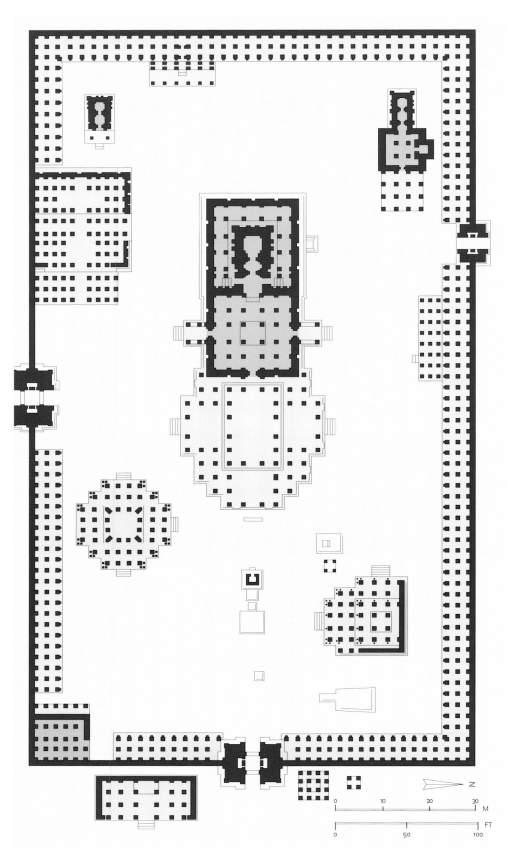

**Plan of the Vitthala Temple
in Hampi**
The Vitthala Temple in Hampi is
dedicated to an *avatar* of Vishnu
and is one of the largest buildings
constructed by the Vijayanagara
dynasty. It was commissioned by
Krishnadeva Raya, who reigned
during the first third of the sixteenth century. Its rectangular
plan measures 165 by 100 m, and is
surrounded by a triple portico on
granite pillars; access is via three
gopurams. The sanctum and its
square *mandapa* are preceded by a
vast *ardha-mandapa* open on all
sides. The secondary buildings,
including a little *ratha*, a building
in the form of a processional chariot (page 201), and small cruciform
buildings, are all constructed in
granite. The plan is clearly
inspired by that of Thanjavur
(page 90).

The Vijayanagara style in the Vitthala precinct

A cruciform pavilion with granite pillars set within the precinct of the Vitthala Temple in Hampi. The Vijayanagara style contrives to be both light and ornate.

Technical virtuosity at the Vitthala Temple

Each pillar with its four surrounding colonnettes and four little lions that form the base of the compound support was carved from a monolith. The stone-carvers of Hampi were indeed true virtuosi.

the Khajuraho statuary or of that of the Venugopala Temple. The figures are somewhat sentimental, and the embracing couples (*mithunas*) possess a showy vulgarity.

Behind this first wall, a second and considerably smaller *gopuram* leads through
into the huge courtyard within which stands the temple itself. Granite porticoes are
set around the outside of a peripheral passageway enclosing a huge dance pavilion
(*mandapa*). The portico is clearly designed for circumambulation. The hypostyle
mandapa is entirely supported by monolithic pillars. At the back of this courtyard, a
very low sanctum is crowned by a very modest *shikhara*, in striking contrast with the
enormous towers of the *gopurams* of the outer enclave.

The pillars of the portico are also monolithic, and at their base are emblematic
lions of the kind first encountered in the art of the Pallavas some seven centuries
earlier; they are found at both Mamallapuram and Kanchipuram. Here, however, the
style is more 'expressionistic' and does not aspire to realism.

The Vitthala Temple was built by the munificent King Krishnadeva Raya
(1509–1530) and is consecrated to the god Vithoba, who is a manifestation of
Vishnu. A series of meticulous restoration programmes has brought new life to its
ruins. Of particular interest in this complex is the granite temple, with its extraordinary pillars against which are rearing elephants mounted by child mahouts. Each

elephant is surmounted by a *makara* and is integrated with the pillar on which it rests.

Accomplished as this carving may seem, it is exceeded in virtuosity by the monolithic groups of four slender colonnettes resting on a square base made up of four seated lions. These apparently frail supports carved from solid granite carry a remarkably elegant roof with wide, overhanging eaves.

Immediately in front of the Vitthala Temple stands a smaller-scale shrine built in imitation of a *ratha*, or ceremonial chariot, with four stone wheels that we can almost believe rotate on their axles. In this we see again the transposition into stone of the great ritual juggernauts, those wooden chariots used in processions that 'beat the bounds' of the town.

In the vast extent of the ruins at Hampi, the visitor here and there comes across little hypostyle shrines with finely sculpted pillars. Each is a place of worship and each is crowned by a relatively low *shikhara* in the form of a tower of successively receding storeys. The extreme hardness of the granite from which they are built and carved makes these delicate works the more surprising. Everywhere there are low reliefs displaying processions of elephants, lions or peacocks, while the refinement shown in the outline of these buildings demonstrates the subtle aesthetic and exquisite lifestyle of the Vijayanagara court.

That way of life was destroyed in the collapse of the empire, after the battle of Talikota in 1565. The end of the Vijayanagara empire was not, however, the end of Hinduism, which retained its powerful hold on the Indian mind. The Vijayanagara style was inherited by the Hindu Nayak dynasty, which not merely preserved it but brought it to still greater perfection.

A surviving oratory
In the immense field of ruins left by the Muslim invaders at Hampi are to be found a number of almost intact temples. Built in granite and with monolithic columns, they exhibit a remarkable lightness of structure.

The Processional Chariots

A juggernaut
In the great Arunachaleshvara Temple at Tiruvannamalai (early sixteenth century) stands this extraordinary processional chariot of sculpted wood. It is mounted on axles with solid wheels and used to carry the divine images through the streets of the city on processional days. Hauled and propelled by dozens of men, these wooden vehicles reflect ancient forms of construction and offer us an insight into a form of technology in wood that is still alive today.

Among the forms of worship practised by Hindus, one of the more notable involved magnificent processions that circled the temple. During the major festivals of the god worshipped in the temple, the divine statues were removed from the gloom of their sanctum and drawn around the temple in the presence of the multitudes. This was a rite of circumambulation conferring sanctity, and the participants in such manifestations of the power of the divinity were thought to incur a share of that sanctity.

In India, the processions required huge wooden chariots or *rathas*. These movable monuments give an idea of how religious buildings of stone and wood continued to be related. They were up to 5 or 6 m in height and could weigh several tonnes, with enormous wheels (whose diameter could be more than 2 m) made of solid wood. Their profusely decorated sides included rows of sculpted gods and made the chariots veritable movable temples. The ornamentation generally included scenes from the legends of the divinity.

Vestiges of a rich traditional art
Detail of the divine images decorating the sides of a south Indian processional chariot. These chariots, built from wood and assembled in traditional fashion, are a kind of 'living fossil', invaluable to the historian of stone architecture.

Pages 202–203
The great temple of Tiruvannamalai
The Arunachala Temple (early six-teenth century) is dedicated to Shiva 'of the fiery linga' and do-minated by a rocky hill on whose summit, on festival days, a beacon is lit in honour of the sun. The temple complex's eight *gopurams* and double-walled precinct are typical of the architecture of Tamil Nadu. In the foreground is a vast tank for ritual ablutions.

A city of grids
A view over the temple-city of Tiruvannamalai from the top of its highest *gopuram*. The orthogonal layout of the complex, which was built in the sixteenth century by King Krishnadeva Raya, is clearly visible, as are the successive precincts. It is a typical product of south Indian Nayak architecture.

The Apogee of the Dravidian Style

The sixteenth century saw a campaign of temple building in the south of the Dec-can. The result was a wealth of superb gigantic temples with concentric enclosing walls that transform the sanctuary into a huge sacred city analogous to the universe and the mountain ranges that were thought of as its borders. One of the finest examples of this phenomenon is the Tiruvannamalai complex. At its centre stands the Temple of Arunachaleshvara, dedicated to the unchangeable Aruna, or Surya, the Sun, who is considered one of the *avatars* of Shiva.

The temple was begun under the Vijayanagara king Krishnadeva Raya and dates from the early sixteenth century. It was rebuilt and restored after bloody battles between Hindus and Muslims. The temple-city covers some ten hectares and lies at the foot of a rocky outcrop that is, even today, a famous pilgrimage site.

There is something almost unreal about the city of Tiruvannamalai with its eight white *gopurams* that stand out against the hillside and lie reflected in the huge abla-tion tank at their feet. The eight successive levels of the four external gateways rise to more than 60 m in height. From their top, the whole complex, arranged around its two orthogonal axes, illustrates a vision of the world: it is a veritable cosmic *man-dala*, a 'radiant city' that seems to foreshadow the divine world amid a luxuriant and brightly coloured natural landscape.

There are enormous white *gopurams* at Kanchipuram too, where they punctuate the enclosure of the Shri Ekambareshvara Temple built in 1506, again by Krishnadeva Raya. Dedicated to Shiva in his aspect of 'sky-clad' ascetic, it comprises a tank sur-rounded by a portico, with an islet at its centre that marks the centre of the universe.

The impression of immensity conveyed by these two sites is confirmed at the Ran-ganatha complex at Tiruchirapalli (Trichy). This is a Vaishnavite sanctuary in which the cosmic god is venerated, and it has no less than seven concentric enclosures.

In the same city, the Jambukeshvara Temple, on the island of Shrirangam, is con-secrated to Shiva in his aspect as Lord of the island Jambudvipa, which is the centre of seven islands known in Indian cosmology. Here, though there are only five con-centric precincts, the scale is more impressive still. The seven *gopurams* are painted in vivid colours; their façades reproduce the now conventional miniature buildings, whose successive levels form 'celestial hierarchies'. Their steep sides and swarming decoration of *rathas* and polychrome stucco statues are vertiginous and an apt metaphor for the celestial city.

The same impression of infinity is given by the corridors intended for internal processions; their fascinating perspectival effects seem to continue to vanishing point. The colossal dimensions are a reminder that these concentric circumambula-tion routes were once trodden by elephants. Their innumerable granite pillars, sur-mounted by lions with terrifying fang-like tongues, are typical of Tamil architecture of the seventeenth and eighteenth centuries.

Wooden floors at Tiruvannamalai
A view vertically upwards through the successive storeys of wooden floors in the great *gopuram* at Tiruvannamalai.

Towers defending the temple at Tiruvannamalai
The ten-storey west *gopuram* of Tiruvannamalai is preceded by a smaller gateway on the edge of the tank. These high towers – the further from the sanctum, the higher they are – symbolise the mountain ranges that border the universe in Hindu cosmology.

The centre of the world
The little pavilion occupying the centre of the tank in the Temple of Ekambareshvara (1506) at Kanchipuram has a cosmological significance: it symbolises the centre of the universe surrounded by the primordial waters.

A six-headed vision at Kanchipuram
Detail of the very late ornament of the Ekambareshvara Temple at Kanchipuram, dedicated to Shiva as Lord of Asceticism. This is the six-headed Kartikeya, son of Shiva, riding on the peacock. According to legend, Kartikeya multiplied his head when six women were arguing about who would bring him up.

Page 207
A monumental *gopuram* at Kanchipuram
The impressive silhouette of the great *gopuram* giving access to the Ekambareshvara Temple at Kanchipuram. This colossal gate, which is more than 60 m high, is the work of the Nayak king Krishna-deva Raya (1509–1530). As a patron of architecture he sought to efface the trail of destruction left by the Muslim invaders.

The holy city of Shrirangam
At Tiruchirapalli (Trichy), the vast temple-city of Ranganatha on the island of Shrirangam is a Vaishnavite sanctuary dedicated to the 'Lord of the Universe'. Its numerous successive walled precincts are marked by twenty-one *gopurams*.

The lion effigy
The animal pillar carved from granite is one of the characteristics of Nayak architecture. This one is from the Ranganatha complex at Tiruchirapalli (seventeenth century).

A protective image at Tiruchirapalli

The Jambukeshvara Temple at Tiruchirapalli is another vast temple surrounded by walled precincts and entered through a series of *gopurams*. It is dedicated to Shiva under the auspices of the *jambuka*, the tree that grows in Paradise. Mounting guard over the entrance to this sacred complex are the great *gopurams* with their protective monsters.

The concave *gopurams* of Tamil India

Unlike the convex towers of the Nagara style in Bhubaneshwar, Tamil *gopurams* are concave in profile, giving greater emphasis to the surging verticality of these enormous buildings. Some of them have fifteen storeys with each successive one narrower than that below. This is the great *gopuram* of the Jambukeshvara Temple at Tiruchirapalli, built by a Nayak king of Madurai in the seventeenth century.

The city of the gods represented at Tiruchirapalli
Detail of the miniature buildings decorating the main *gopuram* of the Jambukeshvara Temple at Tiruchirapalli (Trichy). Their vivid colours derive from the traditional colour decoration of temples and sculptures and are intended to evoke the cosmic mountain. Like the *shikhara* rising above the sanctum of the temple, the *gopuram* symbolises the Himalayan 'Pleasure Mountain' of Shiva, the dwelling of the gods.

The four precincts of the Jambukeshvara Temple
The Temple of Jambukeshvara was built on the island of Shrirangam, at Tiruchirapalli during the Nayak period. Its four walled precincts contain both religious and civil buildings. The complex is rigorously axial and symmetrical. In the later monuments of Hinduism, the hypostyle hall reaches prodigious dimensions.

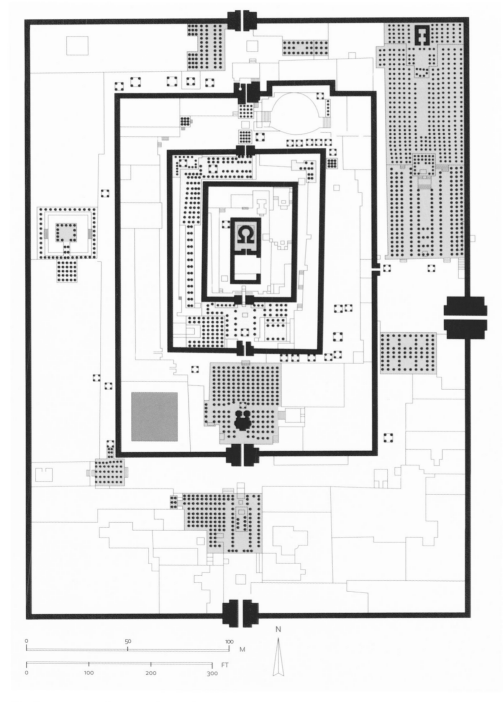

**The pyramidal *gopuram* at
Tiruchirapalli**
The projecting central element
of the south *gopuram* in the Jambukeshvara Temple at Tiruchirapalli is an epitome of *gopuram*
architecture. On either side of the
central bays stand the *dvarapalas*,
or guardians. They are flanked by
symmetrical miniature temples.
Architecture and brightly coloured
sculpture are thus fused in a manner typical of the Hindu temples
of Tamil Nadu.

Composite supports in Nayak temples

The galleries by which later Tamil temples are surrounded rest on composite supports. In the temple at Shrirangam, this system comprises two juxtaposed columns. The larger of them carries the heavy lintels, while the slender one supports the weight of a sitting lion on which the corbelled cross-beams rest.

A processional way at the Jambukeshvara Temple

Perspective effect in a broad covered gallery at the Jambukeshvara Temple in Tiruchirapalli (seventeenth century). The granite pillars support the corbelled ceiling. These porticoes were designed for festivals, when the ritual of circumambulation around the sanctum took the form of processions that often included elephants.

Madurai

The historic capital of southern India, the centre of Tamil Nadu and its art metropolis, the temple-city of Madurai is the example of an aesthetic not averse to tropical luxuriance. The Minakshi Sundareshvara Temple is dedicated to Shiva; beside him sits the 'fish-eyed goddess', an ancient local divinity equated with Parvati, Shiva's consort. The site was already known to Roman historians and geographers – it is mentioned by Strabo and Ptolemy – and had long been famous in its own right; it had already seen centuries of uninterrupted worship by the time the present temple was constructed. This was decreed by Tirumala Nayak (1623–1659), a Croesus-like sovereign of the Dravidian Nayak dynasty, who fought tooth and nail to ensure the survival of Hindu culture in Madurai. He was a king of great magnificence and created in Madurai a kind of repository of the Tamil artistic and religious heritage.

The double temple in which Shiva and Minakshi are worshipped here was built on two parallel east–west axes. The rectangular precinct of 254 by 237 m covers six hectares and has eleven enormous towers. The high external wall is interrupted by the four *gopurams* erected on the axes of the temple of Shiva. The monumental towers have eleven storeys and attain a height of over 60 m; their silhouette, with its concave corner-profile, creates an irresistible upward dynamic.

The tank at Madurai
The great Minakshi Sundareshvara Temple (1623–1659), dedicated to Shiva and his wife, is a vast temple-city in southern India. It is a double temple, with two *garbha grihas* in two parallel courtyards. At the heart of the complex, the large tank is surrounded by steps and sheltered by a granite portico. In the background, one of the axial *gopurams* of the temple.

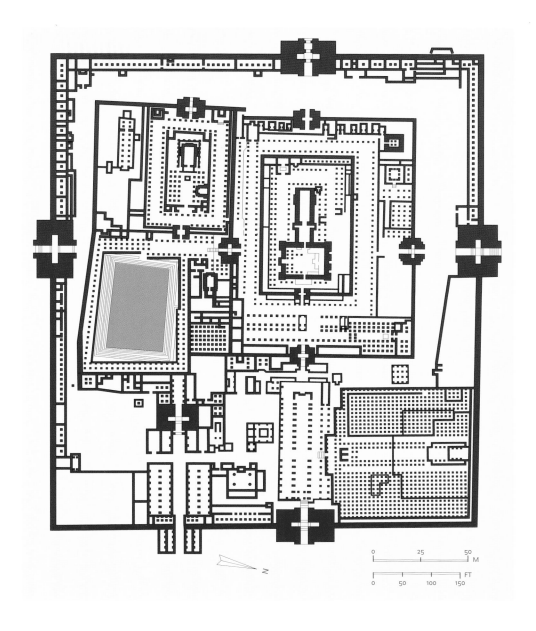

It is one of the paradoxes of the architectural development of Hindu temples
that the vertical forms are slowly transformed. At Bhubaneshwar, the *shikharas*
were of convex profile, emphasised by the hyperbolic curves of the corner-profiles;
in the Nayak buildings of southern India, the concave profile accentuates still further the vertical thrust of the *gopurams*.

From the time of the very first temple gates, at the Kailasa Temple at Ellora and
the Pallava temples at Kanchipuram and Thanjavur, the summit of the *gopuram* had
displayed a barrel-vault shape. The end section of this forms a wide horseshoe arch,
and in this we recognise the *kudu* motif with all its symbolic implications.

Entering by the south *gopuram* of the Minakshi Sundareshvara Temple, the
visitor sees, to the right, the huge tank known as the Golden Lotus Lake. It is surrounded by steps, so that the seasonal changes in water-level do not affect the pilgrim's access to ritual ablution. The tank is 50 m long and in its green waters are
clearly reflected the granite pillars making up the colonnade that runs all around it.

In the north-east corner of the complex, the thousand-pillared hall or *mandapa*
(it actually numbers 985 pillars!) contains the sanctuary dedicated to Nataraja
or Nateshvar, the Lord of the Dance, Shiva in cosmic form. A labyrinthine space,
the hall is rather low relative to its surface area of 70 by 75 m, that is, over 5 000 m².
All its hundreds of pillars are granite monoliths.

The city of the gods reflected at Madurai
The slightly concave profiles of the tall *gopurams* at Madurai swarm with uncounted divinities, *apsaras* and *dvarapalas*. This supernatural population represents the Hindu pantheon in its Himalayan dwelling place, the Mount Kailasa of Shivaism. In the background stands the east *gopuram*.

The structure of the cosmic mountain
Transverse section of one of the great *gopurams* at Madurai (seventeenth century), with its nine or so storeys. The floors rest on wooden beams.

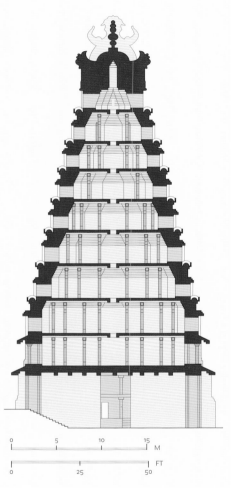

Page 217
End section of the summit of a *gopuram*
The terrifying visage of a monster is there to protect the temple. Beneath him, an assembly of praying wise men surround the lion-masks that form a halo to the emblem of the god. Above the white Nandi bulls of Shiva are two gigantic *dvarapalas*. Between them is the door to a miniature oratory, with its own guardians flanking the entrance.

A riot of vivid colours
The crowds of gods – Shiva, Parvati and Durga – 'saints' and ascetics, or *sadhus*, that proliferate on the successive storeys of the Madurai *gopurams* are all lovingly painted in striking colours. Their polychrome brilliance is revived after each monsoon. The architectonic elements of each storey evoke the miniature buildings of Hindu tradition, while the rows of *kudus* (below) symbolise the windows through which the divinities look down to earth from their dwelling.

The Lord of the Dance
Within a halo of flames, Nataraja, the dancing Shiva, presides over the cosmic order. He is seen here amid the architectural ornaments of a Madurai *gopuram*. Though the stucco sculpture of Madurai is stylistically inferior to medieval statuary, the vivid colours of these statues appeal to the emotions of the faithful.

These are decorated with carvings of animals – elephants, lions or legendary monsters – that are repeated on dozens and even hundreds of pillars; their silhouettes are repeated endlessly down the interminable maze of corridors, processional avenues and sanctuaries in a manner that is typical of the Vijayanagara style, as we have seen exemplified at Hampi. The impression given by the Nayak art of southern India is of overwhelming profusion.

As for the main Minakshi Sundareshvara Temple (1623–1659), it is set within a series of concentric walls, as is the cella of the temple's co-dedicatee. The interior of the sanctuary is a complex mass of interconnecting secondary sanctuaries. On all sides, devotees come to honour the god with their offerings of flowers and incense and to anoint the lingams of Shiva with milk and ghee; from all sides comes the sound of prayers and incantations.

The great sanctuary at Madurai is truly a temple-city. To it come the faithful in their thousands; all the castes of India mingle there with the rural India of the Tamil lands.

Left
Celestial charms
Besides the miniature buildings, the wives of the gods, too, have a prominent place in the decoration of the *gopurams* of the great Temple of Minakshi and Shiva at Madurai. They symbolise the vital energy of sexual attraction.

Centre
Repugnant monsters
Just as the allure of celestial eroticism has a place in the Hindu pantheon, so too, do monstrous and terrifying – indeed demonic – beings; for they are an expression of the duality of the universe, in which creation and destruction alternate.

Right
Patron and protector of authors
Seated on an enormous rat, the plump and placid god Ganesha with his elephant head is found everywhere on the *gopurams* of Madurai. He is considered the son of Shiva, the personification of wisdom and is the patron of literary endeavours.

Omnipresent Polychrome

The architectural decoration of the Nayak epoch is, if possible, even more integral to its monuments than that of any other period of Hindu architecture. This is true not only of the sculpture itself but also of the vivid colours in which the monuments and statues are painted. The temples of the sixteenth to the eighteenth centuries illustrate the progressive invasion of architecture by colour.

The great *gopurams* of the temples of Tiruchirapalli and Madurai are suffused with the gaudiest of colours, all regularly restored after a certain number of monsoon seasons has reduced their brilliance.

The immense surfaces of the towers are covered in dazzling colours. Each of the successive storeys of the *gopurams* of the Minakshi Temple is densely covered in statues: scenes of divinities disporting themselves with their acolytes, gesticulating giants, menacing *dvarapalas* (the monstrous guardians of the sacred domain) and gods with five heads and ten arms. Rows of *apsaras* and goddesses with their lascivious swaying hips are found next to the hieratic divinities of the Hindu pantheon, Krishna, Vishnu, Shiva, and accompanied by monsters and terrifying demons.

Everywhere the brash colours neutralise each other in the jostling of violent images and opulent paintwork; the divinities swarm across the sculpted surfaces in a torrent of imaginary beings. The only element of moderation is supplied by the conventional visual language of the symbolic representations and the postures of the various figures.

Within the temple, the colonnades display the same hallucinatory colours. The pillars, with their rampant leonine monsters, are left in their natural colours. The capitals, however, are now apple-green, the brackets bright red with buttercup-yellow lions, the entablatures and lintels are painted strawberry pink or navy blue, the roofs are ornamented with orange rosettes on an ultramarine background alongside bright scarlet divinities, and so on. The colours are strident and omnipresent.

It will be objected that these intense colours are the product of modern restoration. But this is to misunderstand the natural tendencies of Indian art and to react as the purists did who condemned the restoration of Michelangelo's frescoes in the Sistine Chapel. The expression of the sacred is poles away from any notion of modern taste. It is intended to elicit not aesthetic delectation but religious ecstasy.

Within this phenomenal extravagance, the last word is that of illusion. Just as the *mithunas* of Khajuraho astound and disconcert the Westerner with their overt eroticism, so the polychrome painting of Madurai can repel with its crude, refulgent tonalities. The canons of classical art are of little assistance in approaching and comprehending this ecstasy.

The lesson takes three-dimensional form here, in this world of superabundance and repetition symbolising the cycle of birth and death in the cosmic dance. It is present, too, in this visible welling forth of life, and is still further exalted by the flames of the funerary fires, as if in an eternal renewal implicating all being. And these masterpieces of architecture are the interpreters of this vision of the world in their highly exaggerated forms and colours, which aspire to represent the ecstasy of the divine world.

The great galleries of Madurai
Alive with the comings and goings of the faithful, the galleries leading to the Minakshi Sundareshvara Temple at Madurai are lined with monolithic granite pillars, sculpted in the image of monsters, who bear on their shoulders the corbelled roof-structure. Every part of this architecture is painted in the brightest colours.

Page 223
The glory of Ganesha
On the ceiling of the gallery leading to the Minakshi Sundareshvara Temple in Madurai are many images of the elephant-headed god Ganesha, the son of Shiva and Parvati. His head-dresses, positions, many arms, and the consorts with whom he dances provide infinite iconographical variations.

Teeming ornament at Madurai
The vibrant colours, the formal imagination exhibited in the lion-capped pillars and the luxuriant motifs ornamenting the stone roof-beams make the halls and galleries of the Minakshi Sundareshvara Temple at Madurai one of the most exalted expressions of Dravidian religious feeling.

Traditional formulae at Madurai
The portico of slender granite pillars that borders the ablution tank of the great temple at Madurai exhibits techniques inherited without modification from the Vijayanagara kingdom, where they had been adopted from the forms first developed under the Pallava dynasty. The art of the Nayak dynasty of Madurai is wholly at one with the most ancient traditions of Hindu India.

CONCLUSION

The Weight of Tradition

Our circuit of India has covered almost all of central and southern India. What can we conclude from this immersion in the world of Hindu spirituality and sanctuaries? What can we learn from our study of sacred buildings large and small, from dance pavilion and cella, tiny shrine and vast temple-city?

Two points should be emphasised. First, the stability of the tradition, of symbols handed down from the dawn of time; for example, the continuity of the representation of the temple as cosmic mountain and residence of the gods. Second, the extraordinary permanence of forms and techniques that have remained in service for over a thousand years.

The innovations of the Muslim invader – the keystone and voussoir that effected a revolution in architecture – were very slow to be adopted. Hindu temple architecture in India retained the old methods, which were an inheritance from the time of primitive wooden constructions with thatch roofs, and confined itself to the use of trabeation and corbelling and to heavy roof-structures composed of patterns of stacked stone slabs.

Even after the Sultans' architects had built the mosque of Champaner (1485), with its many domes resting on pillars, Hindu and Jain architects continued to ignore the arch, the vault and the dome. They continued designing the temples at Hampi and Madurai with expensive, labour intensive and traditional corbelled roofs. It is as though acknowledging and adopting technical progress in architecture would have constituted a denial of the entire past; as though, more even than texts or rituals, the forms of architecture were the expression of faith, and temples could perpetuate the occult powers and ancestral magic of their plans, and their *yantras* and *mandalas* could form a bastion against change. It is as if the heavy roof-slabs laid on sturdy pillars could confer on the temple a stability analogous to the unchanging world of the gods.

For it seems that sacred architecture is the only form in which the ancestral practices and myths could be preserved from the great cycle in which birth and death perpetually succeed one another in a world of multiple castes and multiple divinities. In the swarming idols of the Hindu temple, the profusion of the Hindu pantheon is asserted against the aniconic cult of Islam. And the great hymn of birth-agony and death-agony, of creation and destruction, by which the *dharma* is accomplished, is summed up in their dense ranks.

Religious architecture is the reflection of a faith, a way of thought, a mentality. With transformation comes the risk of degradation. Its forms are fixed by the symbols they convey, till they become the most intimate expression of an entire civilisation.

CHRONOLOGICAL TABLE

The great Buddhist *stupa* at Sanchi

Monuments

		800–500 B.C.	500 B.C.–1 B.C.

3rd century Cave-temple at Lomas Rishi
2nd century Jain cave-temples at Kanheri and
Udayagiri
Bhaja: *chaitya*
1st century Sanchi: *stupa* (Buddhist)
Buddhist cave-temple at Karle

c. 1600   Destruction of the cities of
Harappa and Mohenjo-daro
c. 1500 (?)   Vernacular housing built by
pastoral tribes

800–500 B.C.
The Dawn of Time

500 B.C.–1 B.C.
The Earliest Architecture

Events

c. 1600   Earliest Vedic texts written
in Vedic
c. 1300   The Aryas (Indo-Europeans)
invade India
c. 1100   Aryas using iron
c. 1000   The four social classes of the
Aryas established
900–400   *Upanishads* composed
c. 800   End of Aryan migrations
6th century   Life of Buddha and Mahavira
The rise of Buddhism and Jainism

329–325   Alexander the Great in Bactria
and on the banks of the Indus
322–185   Maurya dynasty
269–232   Reign of Ashoka
Ashoka imposes Buddhism
from 180   Demetrios King of Bactria
180–166   Demetrios's campaigns in India
c. 70   End of presence of Greeks in Bactria and India

Façade of a Buddhist *chaitya*
at Ajanta

Interior of a Buddhist *chaitya* at
Ellora

The Bhima Ratha at Mamallapuram

Interior of the Ladh Khan Temple
at Aihole

6th century	Elephanta: Rock-cut Temple
c. 578	Hindu cave-temple (Cave 3) at Badami
late 6th c.	Ellora: Cave 21
c. 600	Badami: Malegitti Shivalaya Temple
c. 600–650	Aihole: Hindu Ladh Khan Temple
630	Mamallapuram: the *rathas*
c. 675–725	Aihole: Durga Temple
7th century	Ellora: last Buddhist rock-cut temples
late 7th c.	Bhubaneshwar: Parashurameshvara Temple

1st century	Nasik: rock-cut *chaitya*
2nd century	Kanheri: *chaitya*
5th century	Ajanta: earliest Buddhist *chaityas* and *viharas*
5th century	Sanchi: Temple 17

700	Mamallapuram: Shore Temple
700–720	Kanchipuram: Kailasanatha Temple
725	Pattadakal: Sangameshvara Temple
745	Pattadakal: Mallikarjuna and Virupaksha Temples
750	Kanchipuram: Vaikuntha Perumal Temple
757–773	Ellora: Kailasa Temple (Cave 16)

A.D. 1–500
The First Great Monuments

A.D. 500–700
The Formation of Styles

A.D. 700–800
The Period of Innovation

1st century	Indo-Scythian Kushana Empire in northern India
144–172	Reign of Kanishka favours Buddhism
	Expansion of Buddhism and Hinduism into Sri Lanka and Indochina
320–575	Gupta dynasty in the Ganges basin
c. 320	King Chandragupta Maurya comes to the throne

500–888	Chalukya dynasty of Vatapi (Badami)
	Emergence of Tantrism
	Shivaism increasingly popular
566–894	Pallava dynasty in southern India
606–647	Harsha King of Kanauj
700–728	Reign of Nrisimhavarman II Rajasimha (Pallava)

8th century	Hinduism increasing
733–746	Vikramaditya II at Pattadakal (Chalukya)
750–984	Ganga dynasty of Karnataka
754–982	Rashtrakuta dynasty in the Deccan

The Durga Temple at Aihole

Detail of the hypostyle hall of the
Rock-cut Temple at Elephanta

The Mukteshvara Temple at
Bhubaneshwar

late 9th c. Khajuraho: Chaunsath Yogini
Temple
9–10th c. Ellora: Jain rock-cut Indra
Sabha Temple (Cave 32)
950–1000 Bhubaneshwar: Mukteshvara
Temple
954 Khajuraho: Lakshmana Temple
10–11th c. Chola bronze masterpieces
c. 1000 Thanjavur: Brihadishvara Temple

1000–1100 Bhubaneshwar: Rajarani Temple
c. 1020 Khajuraho: Kandariya Mahadeva
Temple
1032–1045 Mount Abu: Jain Vimala Vasahi
Temple
c. 1050 Bhubaneshwar: Lingaraja Temple
c. 1075 Bhubaneshwar: Brahmeshvara
Temple
late 10th c. Nagda: Sasbahu Temples
1117 Belur: Chennakeshava Temple
1150 Halebid: Hoysaleshvara Temple

The Surya Temple at Konarak

c. 1240 Konarak: Surya Temple
13th c. Ranakpur: Surya Temple
1230 Mount Abu: Luna Vasahi Temple
1268 Somnathpur: Keshava Temple
13th c. Tiruchirapalli: Venugopala Temple
1397 Belur: *gopuram* of Chennakeshava
Temple

A.D. 800–1000
The Great Artistic Flowering

836–1267 Chola dynasty
916–1250 Chandella dynasty at Khajuraho
950–1002 Reign of Dhanga (Chandella)
973–1190 Chalukya dynasty of Kalyani
985–1014 Thanjavur: Reign of Rajaraja I

The *shikhara* of the Brihadishvara
Temple at Thanjavur

A.D. 1000–1200
The Period of the Masterworks

1017–1029 Reign of Vidyadhara at Khajuraho
1020–1342 Hoysala dynasty in the mid-
Deccan
1076–1568 Ganga dynasty in Orissa
1142–1220 Sena dynasty in Bengal
1186 Muhammad of Ghor raids Lahore
and Delhi

A.D. 1200–1400
The Muslim Onslaught

1202 End of Hindu Empire in Bengal
1206 Foundation of the Delhi Sultanate
1221 Moghuls attack northern India
1308–1312 Conquest of the Deccan by the
Sultans of Delhi
1327 Muslims conquer the Hoysala
kingdom
1334–1736 Nayak dynasty in southern India
1336–1565 Vijayanagara dynasty, whose
capital is Hampi
1343 Reconquest of the Hoysala
kingdom

The Kandariya Mahadeva Temple
at Khajuraho

The *mandapa* of the Adinatha
Temple at Ranakpur

1439 Ranakpur: Jain Adinatha Temple
1506 Kanchipuram: Ekambareshvara
Temple
c. 1520 Hampi: Vitthala and Pampapati
Temples
early 16th c. Tiruvannamalai: Arunachaleshvara
Temple (restored 17th century)

16th c. Jain complex at Palitana
17th c. Tiruchirapalli: Jambukeshvara and
Ranganatha Temples
1623–1659 Madurai: Sundareshvara Temple
dedicated to Shiva and Minakshi

Monuments

A.D. 1400–1700
The Hindu Reawakening

A.D. 1400–1700
The Hindu Reawakening

Events

1509–1530 Reign of Krishnadeva Raya, great
builder of Vijayanagar
1510 Goa founded by Alfonso Albu-
querque
1565 Battle of Talikota: Hampi is cap-
tured and sacked

1623–1659 Reign of Tirumala Nayak
1640 Foundation of Madras
1674 French established at Pondicherry
British established at Calcutta

The *mandapa* of the Vimala Vasahi
Temple at Mount Abu

Gallery of the Jambukeshvara
Temple at Tiruchirapalli

Glossary

Abacus: Upper part of a capital.

Amalaka: Horizontal disk with lateral ribs set at the top of a temple tower in northern India.

Apsara: Celestial nymph often found among the carvings decorating a temple.

Aranyakas: Texts explaining acts of mythical or ritual kind, which give special energy and are only known by insiders.

Ardha-mandapa: Small pillared hall preceding the → *mandapa* as a form of vestibule to the temple. Known as *antarala* in a special kind of northern-temple style (→ *Bogha-mandapa*).

Arya: Indo-European people who invaded northern India around the second millennium B.C.

Atman: Principle of the individual, the 'self'. In antithesis with → *brahman*.

Avatar: Incarnation of a deity. In Hinduism, Krishna, like → Buddha, is regarded as an avatar of Vishnu.

Bogha-mandapa, Bogha-mandira: Hall in which offerings were made; precedes a → Nagara or northern-style temple.

Brahma: One of the three original divinities of Hinduism.

Brahman: In → Vedism, refers to the principle of prayer, later the neutral concept, soul of the world, highest principle; in its antithesis with → *atman*, fundamental to Hindu philosophical debate.

Brahmanas: Texts explaining → Vedic rites and sacrifice but also legends and philosophical considerations.

Brahmins: Members of the highest Hindu caste; one of the four social categories or → *varnas*, that of the priesthood, which was responsible for rites and sacrifice.

Buddha: Name given to the 'Enlightened One', who has attained spiritual enlightenment. Siddhartha Gautama, founder of the Buddhist doctrine, lived during the second half of the sixth century A.D.

Buddhism: Religious doctrine preached by → Buddha.

Candrashala: Northern Indian term for → *kudu*.

Cella: Latin term for the sanctum of a temple; → *garbha griha*

Chaitya: Buddhist prayer hall, with apsidal ending; the barrel-vault forms the *chaitya* arch, referred to in its outline form as the → *kudu*.

Chalukya: Medieval dynasty of southern India.

Chandella: Medieval dynasty of the north of the Deccan; its capital was Khajuraho.

Chola: Medieval dynasty of southern India, whose capital was Thanjavur.

Circumambulation: Ritual by which the devotee walks clockwise around the temple or other holy edifice.

Contrapposto: Italian term for the position of a standing figure resting the weight on one leg, with the other leg slightly bent. The hip that bears the weight is therefore out of centre.

Corbel: A projecting architectural member supporting a weight.

Corbelling: Courses built out beyond one another to support vaults or domes or, more generally, roofs. In the Hindu technique of roofing, a stone corbel is placed across each corner of the orthogonal roof-space, creating a smaller orthogonal space at 45° to the first. Further sets of four corbels are put with their ends on the four below until the space left to be spanned is small enough to be covered by a slab of stone, which seals off the pyramidal roof thus created.

Deul: The name given to the tower or → *shikhara* of a temple, also to the whole layout; especially in north-east India.

Dharma: The → Buddhist or → Brahmanic law governing the universe and, hence, moral law.

Dravidian: The southern Indian architectural style, so called after the group of languages spoken in southern and central India.

Dvarapala: Symbolic guardian of the gates of a → Buddhist, Hindu or → Jain temple.

False lantern dome: One term for the 'domes' made by Hindu architects who, refusing to acknowledge the existence of vaults and domes, used corbelling techniques to achieve similar effects.

Ganga: Goddess; female personification of the River Ganges.

Garbha griha: The sanctum of the temple, also referred to here as the → cella (Latin: room, shrine) by analogy with the shrine of a Greek or Roman temple.

Ghanta kalasha: Emblematic bell-shaped vase set above the → *amalaka* on the roof of a Hindu temple.

Gopi: A cow-girl or milkmaid, especially in connection with the cult of Krishna.

Gopuram: Monumental gateway giving access to a → Dravidian temple precinct.

Gumpha: 'Cave', appears particularly in context with the caves of Orissa.

Hoysala: Dynasty of the southern Deccan; also describes the highly ornamental architectural style typical of this dynasty.

Jagamohana: The name of the → *pita deul* or dance and assembly hall (→ *mandapa*) in Hindu temples of Orissa.

Jain, Jainism: One of the three great religions of India; Jain was founded by → Mahavira, a prophet, also called Jina (the Victorious).

Jali: Obtained by perforating a slab of stone in imitation of lattice work. It is used to block a bay and yet let some light filter into the building.

Jambuka: According to the tradition, trees growing in paradise.

Kailasa: The sacred mountain on which Shiva and his wife Parvati live; the cosmic summit of the universe in the Hindu cosmology.

Kalasha: Emblematic water vessel crowning the tower of a temple.

Karma: The 'account' of a person's actions, which determines whether or not he or she will suffer reincarnation.

Kshatriyas: Second of the four → *varnas;* social category, that of the warriers and rulers.

Kudu: Term for the → *chaitya* arch, which is a barrel-vault seen in section. A decorative motif, often carved with a bust-length figure in it as if at a window. The *kudu* has a symbolic role, referring to the residence of the gods.

Leitmotif: A recurrent theme.

Linga: The symbolic phallus of Shiva, the representation of Shiva commonly found in the sanctum of a Shivaite temple.

Mahadeva: The Great God; epithet of Shiva, sometimes also applied to Vishnu.

Maha-mandapa: Vestibule in southern temple style.

Mahavira: The founder of → Jainism.

Makara: Mythical river monster whose body terminates in foliage rather than a tail; symbol for water and disorder of nature.

Mandala: 'Circle'; symbolic diagram, consisting of circles and rectangles, showing the world in its cosmic development.

Mandapa: Columned hypostyle hall in a Hindu temple, in which the devotees assemble and the ritual dances take place (→ *pita deul*, → *jagamohana*, → *mandira*).

Mandira: Term used of the → *mandapa* of temples in the → Nagara or northern style. (→ *bogha-mandira*, → *nata-mandira*)

Mithuna: Amorous or erotic couple, often sculpted in temple decoration.

Modillion: Small bracket supporting a → corbel or cornice.

Mount Meru: Cosmic mountain symbolising the centre of the earth, surrounded by mountain chains and seas. On it live the divinities of the Hindu pantheon.

Nagara: Sanskrit for 'north', it refers to the architectural style of north-east India.

Nandi: Bull, the 'vehicle' or mount of Shiva.

Naos: Greek term describing the sanctum (Latin: → cella) of a Greek temple.

Nata-mandira: The dance hall of a → Nagara or northern-style temple.

Nataraja: Sanskrit for 'Lord of the Dance', it describes Shiva in his aspect as creator and destroyer of worlds. He is normally represented dancing within a circle of flame.

Nayak: Title of the rulers of southern India (Madurai), in particular in the seventeenth and eighteenth centuries.

Pada: The base of a building. Typical element of the → *shikharas* of eastern Indian temples.

Paga: Vertical projection on a temple tower.

Pallava: Medieval dynasty of southern India.

Pancayatana: Term for a group of five temples or *quincunx*: one central temple and four secondary shrines placed in the coins.

Pidas: Series of superimposed → corbels, typical of the step-pyramid roofs of → *mandapas*, which exhibit horizontal recesses at each corbelled step.

Pita deul: Refers to the meeting or dance pavilion (→ *mandapa*, → *jagamohana*) of a temple.

Pradakshinapatha: Circumambulatory passage around a shrine.

Pronaos: Greek term for the vestibule of a Greek or Roman temple, enclosed by walls at the side and by columns at the front; also describes a temple comprising a *pronaos*.

Raja: Title of the sovereign in southern India.

Ramayana: Great Hindu epic on the legendary hero Rama, who is the seventh incarnation of Vishnu.

Ratha: 1. Chariot in the form of a movable temple for transporting the images of the gods during the processions marking their festivals. The monolithic buildings at Mamallapuram imitate the form of these chariots and are therefore also called *rathas*. 2. Generic name for the projections or → *pagas* on temple towers, which may have arisen because the processional chariot is in the form of the → *shalas* that ornament the roof-storeys of the → Dravidian temple, and form the point about which the projection (→ *paga*) was originally organised.

Rekha (rekha deul): Term for the tower of a temple in Orissa (→ *shikhara*).

Sadhu: Brahmanic ascetic.

Shala: The name for the diminutive → *chaityas* with → *kudu* windows used to decorate the successive roof-storeys of the → Dravidian temple.

Shikhara: The tower of a temple (→ *deul*, → *rekha deul*).

Shthapaka: The architect who designs the plan of a temple according to the ritual requirements.

Shthapati: The architect who executes the plan of the → *shthapaka*.

Shudras: lowest of the four → *varnas*; fourth social category, that of the manual labourers and subordinates, who are not allowed to study → Vedic texts.

Stupa: Funerary mound symbolising the presence and law of → Buddha; may contain relics of the founder.

Stupi: The rounded 'finial' unit of a → Dravidian temple; often used at the corner of the roof-storeys in place of the rectangular → *shala*.

Surasundari: Nymph.

Svastika: Cross in fragmentary squares; symbol of solar movement.

Tantra: Religious writings dealing with symbolism and ritual.

Tantrism: Secret doctrines concerning Hindu ritual, also taken up in certain → Buddhist schools of thought. Founded on the → Tantra and making use of → *mandala* and → *yantra* diagrams, the doctrines prescribe physical practices (→ *yoga*).

Torana: Portal with monolithic or lintelled arch set before a Hindu or → Buddhist holy place.

Trimurti: Image of the trinity of the deities → Brahma, Vishnu and Shiva symbolising the three aspects: creation, preservation and destruction.

Triratha: A → *shikhara* with three → *rathas* or projecting elements (→ *pagas*).

Trikutashala: Triple shrine or three-celled temple.

Tumulus: Latin term describing an artificial mound of earth or stone marking a tomb.

Tympanum: Space over a door between the lintel and the arch or space forming the centre of a pediment.

Upanishads: Texts concerning theological and philosophical considerations.

Vaishyas: third of the four → *varnas*; social category of the farmers and merchants.

Varna: Generic term for the four great social categories in the → Vedic society (→ Brahmins, → Kshatriyas, → Vaishyas and → Shudras); out of them grew the Indian caste system.

Vedas: Term describing the four great sacred 'texts' of Brahmanism, written in Vedic in the second and third millennia B.C.: *Atharva-Veda, Yajur-Veda, Rig-Veda, Sama-Veda*.

Vedika: Post-and-rail-type of stone balustrade or low wall encircling a temple.

Vesara: Style intermediate between → Dravidian and → Nagara styles.

Vihara: Term for → Buddhist monastery.

Vina: Ancient Indian musical instrument with one or more strings; a kind of lute.

Yantra: Symbolic and mystic diagram referring to a deity. In → Tantrism, used to stimulate meditation.

Yoga: Physical discipline intended to liberate the spirit through mastery of movement and breathing.

Yogini: 'Working energy'. Women practising asceticism.

BIBLIOGRAPHY

Acharya, Prasanna Kumar: *Dictionary of Hindu Architecture*, London, 1995.

Archaeological Survey of India, The Annual Reports, Calcutta / New Delhi, 1902–1938.

Ayyar, Jagadisa: *South Indian Shrines*, Madras, 1922.

Basham, Arthur Llewellyn: *The Wonder that was India*, 2 vols., London, 1987 (4th edition, London, 1995).

Brown, Percy: *Indian Architecture, Buddhist and Hindu Periods*, Bombay, 5th edition 1965.

Bussagli, Mario: *Oriental Architecture*, 2 vols., London, 1989.

Chihara, Daigoro: *Hindu-Buddhist Architecture in Southeast Asia*, Leiden / New York / Cologne, 1996.

Choisy, Auguste: *Histoire de l´Architecture*, Paris, 1991.

Dagens, Bruno (ed.): *Mayamatam: Treatise of Housing, Architecture & Iconography*, 2 vols., New Dehli, 1994.

Daniélou, Alain: *Hindu Polytheism*, London / Princeton, 1964.

Daniélou, Alain: *Le Temple hindou*, Paris, 1977.

Dehejia, Vidya: *Indian Art*, London, 1997.

Deva, Krishna: *Temples of India*, 2 vols., New Delhi, 1995.

Doehring, Karl: *Indische Kunst*, Berlin, 1925.

Esnoul, Anne-Marie: L'Hindouisme, in: *Histoire des Religions, Encyclopédie de la Pléiade*, Paris, 1970.

Fischer, Klaus, Michael Jansen and Jan Pieper: *Architektur des indischen Subkontinents*, Darmstadt, 1987.

Flory, Marcel: *Khajuraho*, Paris, 1965.

Franz, Heinrich Gerhard: *Von Gandara bis Pagan. Kultbauten des Buddhismus und Hinduismus in Süd- und Zentralasien*, Graz, 1979.

Frédéric, Louis: *The Temples and Sculptures of Southeast Asia*, London, 1965.

Frédéric, Louis: *The Art of India, Temples and Sculpture*, London, 1959.

Gangoly, Ordhendra Coomar: *Indian Architecture*, Bombay, 1954.

Harle, James Coffin: *The Art and Architecture of the Indian Subcontinent*, Harmondsworth, 1986 (2nd edition, New Haven / London, 1994).

Huntington, Susan L.: *The Art of Ancient India. Buddhist, Hindu, Jain*, New York / Tokyo 1986.

Kramrisch, Stella: *The Art of India through the Ages*, London, 1955.

Kramrisch, Stella: *The Hindu Temple*, 2 vols., Calcutta / London, 1946 (2nd edition, Varanasi, 1980).

Macmillan Dictionary of Art, London, 1997.

Meister, Michael W., M. A. Dhaky and Krishna Dera (eds.): *Encyclopaedia of Indian Temple Architecture (EITA)*, 5 vols., New Dehli, 1983–1996.

Michell, George: *Architecture and Art of Southern India*, Cambridge, 1995 (= New Cambridge History of India; I, 6).

Michell, George: *The Hindu Temple: An Introduction to its Meaning and Forms*, London, 1977 (reprint, Chicago, 1988).

Rambach, Pierre and Vitold de Golish: *The Golden Age of Indian Art: 5th – 13th Century*, Bombay, 1955 (3rd rev. edition, 1967).

Rowland, Benjamin: *The Art and Architecture of India: Buddist, Hindu, Jain*, Harmondsworth, 1953

Schneider, Ulrich: Towards a Sculptural Programme at Elephanta, in: *Investigating Indian Art*, New Dehli, 1970.

Sergent, Bernard: *Genèse de l'Inde*, Paris, 1997.

Shukla, D. N.: *Vastu-Sastra*, 2 vols., New Dehli, 1993–1995.

Sivaramamurti, Calambur: *The Art of India*, New York, 1977.

Soundara Rajan, Kodayanallur V.: *Indian Temple Styles: The Personality of Hindu Architecture*, New Dehli, 1970.

Stierlin, Henri: *Le Monde de l'Inde*, Paris, 1978.

Taddei, Maurizio: *India*, London, 1970.

Tadgell, Christopher: *The History of Architecture in India*, London, 1990.

Viennot, Odette: *Temples de l'Inde centrale et occidentale*, Paris, 1976.

Volwahsen, Andreas: *India*, Fribourg, 1968 (= Architecture of the World, 7).

Zimmer, Heinrich: *Myths and Symbols in Indian Art and Civilization*, Dehli, 1990.

Index – Places

INDEX – Persons

ACKNOWLEDGEMENTS AND CREDITS

The editor, author and photographers would like to thank the institutions and persons that helped to make this volume possible, in particuar:

The Archaeological Survey of India, in New Delhi, and especially R. C. Agrawal, for the authorisations he accorded to the photographers,

Air India, and especially ist representative in Geneva, Jaishree Ramchandran, and Indira Kaczynska, Sales Manager, for the facilities that they made available,

National Museum of India, New Delhi, and the Musée d'Ethnographie, Geneva, for their authorisation to photograph objects in their collections and

Vina Sanyal, Delhi, for the technical organisation of the photographic tour of India.

We are pleased to acknowledge the source of the following documents:

Pages 130, 132–133, 134–135, 137 bottom left, 139, 144, 145 and 164–165: © Thomas Dix.

Our special thanks to Alberto Berengo Gardin for drawing the plans on the following pages: 9, 26, 28, 30, 32, 36, 41, 45, 47, 50, 51, 65, 66, 71, 79, 90, 107, 108, 115, 116, 120, 123, 136, 140, 154, 159, 173, 174, 182, 196, 210, 212, 215 and 216.

ALL 40 TITLES AT A GLANCE
Each book: US$ 29.99 | £ 16.99 | CDN$ 39.95

The Ancient World
▶ The Near East
▶ Egypt
▶ Greece
▶ The Roman Empire
▶ The Greco-Roman Orient

The Medieval World
▶ Byzantium
▶ The Early Middle Ages
▶ The Romanesque
▶ High Gothic
▶ Late Gothic

The Pre-Columbian World
▶ The Maya
▶ Mexico
▶ The Aztecs
▶ Peru
▶ The Incas

Islamic Masterpieces
▶ Islam from Baghdad to Cordoba
▶ Islam from Cairo to Granada
▶ Persia
▶ Turkey
▶ Mogul

The Splendours of Asia
▶ Hindu India
▶ Buddhist India
▶ China
▶ South-East Asia
▶ Japan

Stylistic Developments from 1400
▶ Renaissance
▶ Baroque in Italy
▶ Baroque in Central Europe
▶ Hispanic Baroque
▶ French Classicism

The Modern Age
▶ Neo-Classicism and Revolution
▶ American Architecture
▶ Art Nouveau
▶ Early Modern Architecture
▶ Visionary Masters
▶ Monumental Modern
▶ International Style
▶ Post-Modernism
▶ New Forms
▶ Contemporary Masters

"... a truly remarkable publishing event in architecture."
The Architectural Review
London

▶ Collect 40 volumes of TASCHEN'S WORLD ARCHITECTURE in eight years (1996–2003) and build up a complete panorama of world architecture from the earliest buildings of Mesopotamia to the latest contemporary projects.

▶ The series is grouped into five-volume units, each devoted to the architectural development of a major civilisation, and introducing the reader to many new and unfamiliar worlds.

▶ Each volume covers a complex architectural era and is written so vividly that most readers will feel the urge to go out and discover these magnificent buildings for themselves.

TASCHEN'S WORLD ARCHITECTURE

"An excellently produced, in-formative guide to the history of architecture. Accessible to everyone."
Architektur Aktuell, Vienna

"This is by far the most compre-hensive review of recent years."
Frankfurter Rundschau, Frankfurt

"A successful debut of a very promising series."
Architektur & Wohnen, Hamburg, on *Islam from Baghdad to Cordoba*

"...each theme is presented in a very interesting, lively style... it makes you want to set off straight away to see everything with your own eyes."
Baumeister, Munich, on *The Roman Empire*

▶ TASCHEN'S WORLD ARCHITECTURE presents 6000 years of architectural history in 40 volumes.

▶ Each volume is a detailed and author-itative study of one specific era.

▶ The whole series provides a compre-hensive survey of architecture from antiquity to the present day. Five volumes will be published each year.

▶ TASCHEN'S WORLD ARCHITECTURE is a must for all lovers of architecture and travel.

▶ Renowned photographers have travelled the world for this series, presenting more than 12000 photographs of famous and lesser-known buildings.

▶ Expert authors guide the reader through TASCHEN'S WORLD ARCHI-TECTURE with exciting, scientifically well-founded texts that place architec-ture within the cultural, political and social context of each era.

▶ The elegant, modern design and the clear, visually striking layout guide the reader through the historical and contemporary world of architecture.

▶ Influential architectural theories, typical stylistic features and specific construction techniques are separately explained on eye-catching pages.

▶ Each volume includes between 40 and 50 maps, plans and structural drawings based on the latest scholarly findings and are produced for this series using state-of-the-art computer technology.

▶ The appendix contains clear chronolo-gical tables, giving an instant overview of the correlation between the histor-ical events and architecture of any given civilisation.

▶ A detailed glossary clearly explains architectural terms.

▶ An index of names and places ensures quick and easy reference to specific buildings and people.

▶ Each book contains 240 pages with some 300 color illustrations on high-quality art paper. 240 x 300 mm, hardcover with dust jacket.

Each book: US$ 29.99 | £ 16.99 | CDN$ 39.95